Google Cloud: G Suite Administrator

Google Cloud: G Suite Administrator

Part Number: 093008
Course Edition: 2.0

Acknowledgements

PROJECT TEAM

Author	Media Designer	Content Editor
Laurie A. Perry	Brian Sullivan	Michelle Farney

Logical Operations wishes to thank the members of the Logical Operations Instructor Community, and in particular Jason Latona and Stephen Short, for contributing their technical and instructional expertise during the creation of this course.

Notices

DISCLAIMER

While Logical Operations, Inc. takes care to ensure the accuracy and quality of these materials, we cannot guarantee their accuracy, and all materials are provided without any warranty whatsoever, including, but not limited to, the implied warranties of merchantability or fitness for a particular purpose. The name used in the data files for this course is that of a fictitious company. Any resemblance to current or future companies is purely coincidental. We do not believe we have used anyone's name in creating this course, but if we have, please notify us and we will change the name in the next revision of the course. Logical Operations is an independent provider of integrated training solutions for individuals, businesses, educational institutions, and government agencies. The use of screenshots, photographs of another entity's products, or another entity's product name or service in this book is for editorial purposes only. No such use should be construed to imply sponsorship or endorsement of the book by nor any affiliation of such entity with Logical Operations. This courseware may contain links to sites on the Internet that are owned and operated by third parties (the "External Sites"). Logical Operations is not responsible for the availability of, or the content located on or through, any External Site. Please contact Logical Operations if you have any concerns regarding such links or External Sites.

TRADEMARK NOTICES

Logical Operations and the Logical Operations logo are trademarks of Logical Operations, Inc. and its affiliates.

Google™ and the Google logo are registered trademarks of Google Inc. in the U.S. and other countries. Android™ is a trademark of Google Inc. All other product and service names used may be common law or registered trademarks of their respective proprietors.

Copyright © 2017 Logical Operations, Inc. All rights reserved. Screenshots used for illustrative purposes are the property of the software proprietor. This publication, or any part thereof, may not be reproduced or transmitted in any form or by any means, electronic or mechanical, including photocopying, recording, storage in an information retrieval system, or otherwise, without express written permission of Logical Operations, 3535 Winton Place, Rochester, NY 14623, 1-800-456-4677 in the United States and Canada, 1-585-350-7000 in all other countries. Logical Operations' World Wide Web site is located at **www.logicaloperations.com**.

This book conveys no rights in the software or other products about which it was written; all use or licensing of such software or other products is the responsibility of the user according to terms and conditions of the owner. Do not make illegal copies of books or software. If you believe that this book, related materials, or any other Logical Operations materials are being reproduced or transmitted without permission, please call 1-800-456-4677 in the United States and Canada, 1-585-350-7000 in all other countries.

Google Cloud: G Suite Administrator

Lesson 1: Getting Started with G Suite Administration.....1
Topic A: Create a G Suite Account.. 2
Topic B: Navigate the Admin Console.. 11

Lesson 2: Managing User Accounts..............................21
Topic A: Create and Modify User Accounts................................... 22
Topic B: Use System Roles to Delegate Duties to Users.................. 27
Topic C: Remove and Restore User Accounts................................ 34
Topic D: Manage User Passwords.. 40

Lesson 3: Using Organizational Units............................53
Topic A: Create Organizational Units.. 54
Topic B: Manage G Suite Services with Organizational Units........... 62

Lesson 4: Configuring Drive Storage and Sharing..........71
Topic A: Configure Drive Storage Settings.................................... 72
Topic B: Configure Drive Sharing 84

Lesson 5: Managing Mail Routing, Delivery, and Filtering......97
Topic A: Configure Mail Routing and Delivery..................................98
Topic B: Manage Blacklists and Whitelists.....................................107
Topic C: Filter Messages Based on Compliance Settings.....................111
Topic D: Migrate to G Suite Mail..119

Lesson 6: Working with Google Groups..............................129
Topic A: Create and Modify Groups..130
Topic B: Manage Group Security...143
Topic C: Share Content Using Groups..156
Topic D: Use a Collaborative Inbox..159

Lesson 7: Administering Calendars and Resources.............167
Topic A: Create and Share a Group Calendar..................................168
Topic B: Delegate Calendar Access..173
Topic C: Create and Manage Calendar Resources...........................176

Lesson 8: Configuring and Securing Mobile Devices...........187
Topic A: Set Up Google Mobile Management..................................188
Topic B: Secure Mobile Devices..202

Lesson 9: Using Reporting Tools...211
Topic A: Use Admin Console Reports...212
Topic B: Use Audit Logs...221
Topic C: Troubleshoot Mail Issues...230

Lesson 10: Managing Domain Security and Authentication..239
Topic A: Manage G Suite Domain Security.....................................240
Topic B: Configure 2-Step Verification..245

Appendix A: Mapping Course Content to Google Certified Associate— G Suite Administrator 261

Appendix B: Incorporating Authentication of Your Email 263
Topic A: Incorporate Authentication of Your Email 264

Solutions 267
Glossary 271
Index 275

About This Course

One of the compelling benefits of using G Suite Basic is that you can leave the server hardware management responsibilities to Google. As the administrator of a G Suite domain, you can control the accounts, resources, and apps from a web browser interface. All of your administrative tasks can be accessed from a specialized page, or console, of dashboard controls. From this Admin console, you can perform all the necessary duties of a domain administrator without having to worry about keeping the physical hardware up and running. In this course, you will learn about creating and managing a G Suite domain.

You can also use this course to prepare for the Google Certified Associate—G Suite Administrator certification exam.

Course Description

Target Student

This course is designed for business users or IT professionals who need to set up and administer a G Suite domain by creating and managing users, organizational units, groups, calendars, shared resources, and mobile devices. Managing mail routing and delivery, configuring G Suite apps and services, monitoring account activity and apps usage, and maintaining security are included to facilitate communication and collaboration in a secure environment.

Course Prerequisites

To ensure your success in this course, you should have experience with using a web browser, such as Google Chrome™, and using G Suite. Knowledge of domain administration terminology will be helpful, but not a requirement. You should be familiar with working in a cloud-based productivity suite, such as G Suite. You can obtain this level of skills and knowledge by taking the following Logical Operations courses:

- *Using Google Drive™ and Productivity Apps*
- *Google Cloud Fundamentals*

Course Objectives

In this course, you will set up and manage the G Suite environment for users.

You will:

- Navigate the G Suite Admin console.
- Create and manage user accounts.
- Use organizational units to manage your G Suite environment.
- Configure and implement Drive storage settings and policies.
- Manage mail delivery, routing, and filtering.

- Create groups to share mailboxes and documents, and manage permissions and roles.
- Set up and manage calendar sharing and calendar resources.
- Manage the mobile devices that access your system.
- Use reporting tools to manage usage and security, and to troubleshoot system issues.
- Configure security and authentication policies and methods.

The CHOICE Home Screen

Logon and access information for your CHOICE environment will be provided with your class experience. The CHOICE platform is your entry point to the CHOICE learning experience, of which this course manual is only one part.

On the CHOICE Home screen, you can access the CHOICE Course screens for your specific courses. Visit the CHOICE Course screen both during and after class to make use of the world of support and instructional resources that make up the CHOICE experience.

Each CHOICE Course screen will give you access to the following resources:

- **Classroom**: A link to your training provider's classroom environment.
- **eBook**: An interactive electronic version of the printed book for your course.
- **Files**: Any course files available to download.
- **Checklists**: Step-by-step procedures and general guidelines you can use as a reference during and after class.
- **LearnTOs**: Brief animated videos that enhance and extend the classroom learning experience.
- **Assessment**: A course assessment for your self-assessment of the course content.
- Social media resources that enable you to collaborate with others in the learning community using professional communications sites such as LinkedIn or microblogging tools such as Twitter.

Depending on the nature of your course and the components chosen by your learning provider, the CHOICE Course screen may also include access to elements such as:

- LogicalLABS, a virtual technical environment for your course.
- Various partner resources related to the courseware.
- Related certifications or credentials.
- A link to your training provider's website.
- Notices from the CHOICE administrator.
- Newsletters and other communications from your learning provider.
- Mentoring services.

Visit your CHOICE Home screen often to connect, communicate, and extend your learning experience!

How to Use This Book

As You Learn

This book is divided into lessons and topics, covering a subject or a set of related subjects. In most cases, lessons are arranged in order of increasing proficiency.

The results-oriented topics include relevant and supporting information you need to master the content. Each topic has various types of activities designed to enable you to solidify your understanding of the informational material presented in the course. Information is provided for reference and reflection to facilitate understanding and practice.

Data files for various activities as well as other supporting files for the course are available by download from the CHOICE Course screen. In addition to sample data for the course exercises, the course files may contain media components to enhance your learning and additional reference materials for use both during and after the course.

Checklists of procedures and guidelines can be used during class and as after-class references when you're back on the job and need to refresh your understanding.

At the back of the book, you will find a glossary of the definitions of the terms and concepts used throughout the course. You will also find an index to assist in locating information within the instructional components of the book. In many electronic versions of the book, you can click links on key words in the content to move to the associated glossary definition, and on page references in the index to move to that term in the content. To return to the previous location in the document after clicking a link, use the appropriate functionality in your PDF viewing software.

As You Review

Any method of instruction is only as effective as the time and effort you, the student, are willing to invest in it. In addition, some of the information that you learn in class may not be important to you immediately, but it may become important later. For this reason, we encourage you to spend some time reviewing the content of the course after your time in the classroom.

As a Reference

The organization and layout of this book make it an easy-to-use resource for future reference. Taking advantage of the glossary, index, and table of contents, you can use this book as a first source of definitions, background information, and summaries.

Course Icons

Watch throughout the material for the following visual cues.

Icon	Description
	A **Note** provides additional information, guidance, or hints about a topic or task.
	A **Caution** note makes you aware of places where you need to be particularly careful with your actions, settings, or decisions so that you can be sure to get the desired results of an activity or task.
	LearnTO notes show you where an associated LearnTO is particularly relevant to the content. Access LearnTOs from your CHOICE Course screen.
	Checklists provide job aids you can use after class as a reference to perform skills back on the job. Access checklists from your CHOICE Course screen.
	Social notes remind you to check your CHOICE Course screen for opportunities to interact with the CHOICE community using social media.

1 Getting Started with G Suite Administration

Lesson Time: 1 hour, 30 minutes

Lesson Introduction

As the G Suite account administrator, your first task is setting up and configuring the domain. The configuration process is the same for both large and small organizations. The Admin console and its dashboard contain the majority of the tools you will need so it's important to be familiar with its interface.

Lesson Objectives

In this lesson, you will:

- Sign in and set up a new G Suite account.
- Use the Admin console.

TOPIC A

Create a G Suite Account

The first step in setting up a G Suite account is to define your domain. To ensure that you've thought of everything, it's important to plan the domain names and any organizational units that you might need.

The G Suite Account

A personal Google account gives you access to cloud-based productivity apps, such as Gmail™, Google Calendar™, and Google Drive™. By comparison, a *G Suite* account is an all-in-one solution for your organization that provides access to the same productivity apps, collaboration tools, and services on a subscription basis for everyone in your organization.

Note: On September 29, 2016, Google changed the name of the product from *Google Apps* to *G Suite*. There is additional discussion of the available G Suite editions in the next topic.

Domain Names

A *domain* is a grouping of computers on the Internet based on the nature of their operations. Although there are several types of domains, some of the common ones are commercial, governmental, and educational domains. Domains are identified by their unique names following the period in the web address; for example, .com, .gov, and .edu.

Note: A *naked domain* refers to the domain address being entered in the browser address box without the "www." preceding the domain name. For example, "http://hearthomes.net" is the naked domain for "http://www.hearthomes.net."

A *domain name* is a unique name that identifies a domain on the Internet. Also known as site names, domain names are usually registered by organizations as their website address. In email addresses, the domain name appears after the @ symbol; for example, *admin@mycompany.com*.

When registering with G Suite, you need a *primary domain* that can be either a domain name that you already own or one that you purchase from a Google partner during registration. This is the domain name that will appear in email addresses. It's important to choose your domain name wisely because changing the domain name for an active domain can be challenging. Additionally, the ability to change a domain name depends on how it was purchased. If desired, you can add multiple domains to your Google account.

If your organization has been established for any length of time, you might find it advantageous to use your own domain name instead of purchasing one from Google. This eliminates the need to change your company identity with pre-existing services and clients. However, for organizations that are just getting started, purchasing a domain name from Google can help you with the initial domain setup and connection to Google services.

Domain alias is an alternate name for the primary domain. When created, a domain alias gives users two different email addresses that point to the same mailbox. For example, if the primary domain is *mydomain.com* and the domain alias is *myalias.com*, then mail addressed to jane@mydomain.com or jane@myalias.com will be routed to the same mailbox.

A G Suite account can have multiple domains associated with it as long as you own each of the domain names. For example, when two companies are merged together, both domains would be associated with the same G Suite account and managed by one common administrator. Users at each domain can keep their unique email addresses, but would also share apps and services. However, there are special limitations and restrictions that apply when you add a second domain to your primary domain. More information about secondary domains can be found in the G Suite Administrator Help.

Domain Name Verification

Verifying your domain is the final step in setting up your G Suite account. You need to prove to Google that you own the domain name. If you purchased the domain name directly from Google, then the necessary verification steps have been done for you. If you are using a domain name that you've purchased prior to setting up the domain, the verification steps you follow will depend on the domain host. You might need to consult your network administrator for assistance with this final step of the setup process. You can use any of the following options to verify your domain ownership:

- Add a TXT or CNAME record to your domain's DNS settings at the host's website. This is the recommended method if you have access to your domain's DNS settings.
- Upload an HTML file to your domain's web server. This option is preferred if you don't have access to your domain's DNS settings.
- Add a <meta> tag to the home page of your domain's web server. You must have edit access to the server files.
- If you've purchased your domain name from a Google partner (such as Bluehost® or GoDaddy®), you can give Google permission to interact with your domain host by providing your login credentials and verifying your ownership.

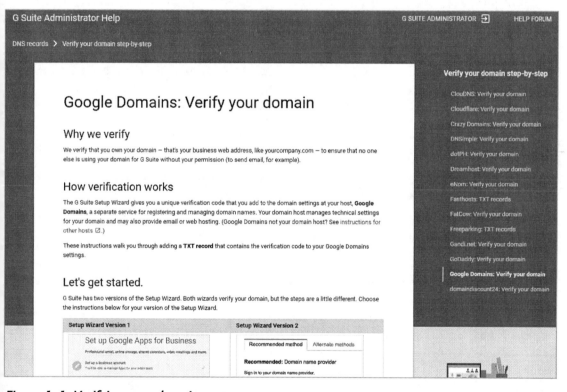

Figure 1-1: Verifying your domain.

Web Addresses

The *web address* identifies the site that has been reserved and assigned to a company, server, or file. A web address has several components. In the sample web address **www.mycompany.com**, mycompany is the domain name that was officially reserved and purchased from a domain registrar. The three letters at the right end of the address indicate the domain, such as .com for commercial.

An *Internet Protocol (IP) address*, such as 198.175.10.4, is a unique address assigned to a computer so that it can communicate with other computers and devices. IP addresses are easily recognized by their dotted decimal notation. Without delving too deep into what each decimal value represents, it's enough for you to know that the decimal values represent the physical network and network host. For some websites, you might see an IP address in the Address bar.

DNS Server

Domain Name System (DNS) is the naming service used on the Internet. For example, the IP address *198.175.10.4* might map to www.google.com. In an organization's network, the IP address *128.4.20.100* might map to Server1. The *DNS Server* is the computer that is running the DNS service used to resolve the DNS names with addresses.

Domain Host

The Internet hosting service that manages and stores your G Suite domain records is called the *domain host*. The records stored on the domain host are necessary for verifying domain ownership, configuring mail, and customizing web addresses. You must work through your domain host to change any of these records.

MX Records

Stored on the DNS server, the *Mail Exchange (MX) record* controls the routing of incoming mail with the Google mail servers. The MX record contains information, such as the address of the destination mail server, the Time To Live (TTL) value in seconds, and record type. Depending on when you purchased your domain, and whether you purchased it through a Google partner, you might need to configure the MX record to point to the Google mail servers. The exact steps to configure your MX record depend on your specific domain host; however, the MX record must contain the correct values to point to the Google servers.

 Note: If you recently purchased your domain while setting up a new G Suite account, Google automatically configured the MX records.

The following MX record values need to be added to your domain's DNS records.

- The **Name/Host/Alias** setting indicates that this record is used for mail addresses.
- By default, the **Time To Live** setting is 3600 seconds, or 1 hour. A recommended TTL value is 86400 so servers are checked every 24 hours for updates.
- The **Priority** setting defines the order of mail delivery. As shown in the following table, the ASPMX.L.GOOGLE.COM server must be set to the highest priority of 1. The priority of the other servers can vary.
- The **Value/Answer/Destination** setting identifies the Google mail server. Some hosts require a period at the end of the server name.

Name/Host/Alias	TTL (in seconds)	Record Type	Priority	Value/Answer/Destination
Blank or @	3600	MX	1	ASPMX.L.GOOGLE.COM
Blank or @	3600	MX	5	ALT1.ASPMX.L.GOOGLE.COM
Blank or @	3600	MX	5	ALT2.ASPMX.L.GOOGLE.COM
Blank or @	3600	MX	10	ALT3.ASPMX.L.GOOGLE.COM
Blank or @	3600	MX	10	ALT4.ASPMX.L.GOOGLE.COM

Billing Plans

G Suite has two billing plans based on the number of user accounts. The total cost is also dependent on the specific G Suite edition that you purchased.

- With the **Flexible Plan**, you are billed monthly for each user account. User accounts can be added or removed at any time, and you pay for the accounts used that month. The service can be canceled at any time without penalty. This type of plan is recommended for smaller organizations with a variable number of employees.
- With the **Annual Plan**, you receive a discounted monthly rate based on an annual commitment of purchased licenses, pro-rated on a monthly basis. You commit to the number of licenses you need, and then add or remove user accounts as desired. If you need to exceed the number of committed licenses, you must buy those extra licenses. You cannot, however, reduce the number of licenses you pay for until the year is up.

Note: The Annual Plan is no longer offered to new customers in the U.S. If you're an existing customer who signed up with an annual plan, then you can continue on that plan. However, if you are new to G Suite, then the Flexible Plan is your only option.

Note: To learn more about how to set up a new Google Apps domain, check out the LearnTO **Use the Google Apps Setup Wizard** presentation from the **LearnTO** tile on the CHOICE Course screen.

Access the Checklist tile on your CHOICE Course screen for reference information and job aids on How to Sign Up for a G Suite Account.

ACTIVITY 1-1
Planning a G Suite Account

Scenario

You've been asked to consult with Building with Heart, a non-profit home construction organization that builds small, two-bedroom homes for qualifying families, about setting up a G Suite account. They want to use G Suite to communicate and collaborate to complete each home-building project. Your organization has four departments: Donations, Construction, Marketing, and Volunteers, with a current staff of 15. While none of the departments has more than five people, you want to have room to grow. Due to the high rate of staff turnover and the number of volunteers, it's important that everyone on staff has the ability to manage and maintain the G Suite domain. You know that it's a major hassle to change the domain name once it's registered, so you want to do some upfront planning.

1. What domain name will you use? Do you currently own the domain name?

2. Will you need to add a secondary domain?

3. Will your domain need organization units within the top-level domain?

4. How many users will you need to register?

ACTIVITY 1-2
Creating a G Suite Business Account

Data File
C:\093008Data\Getting Started with G Suite Administration\Domain.docx

Before You Begin
You own the domain name you will be using during this activity.

Scenario
After planning your domain's structure, you're ready to create the G Suite account for Building with Heart. You own the registered domain name <*your_domain.com*>. As the primary administrator, you'll need to create user accounts. You want to become familiar with the admin interface and learn to navigate your way around it before you ask others to act as your backup.

Note: Activities may vary slightly if the software vendor has issued digital updates. Your instructor will notify you of any changes.

1. Complete the **About You** settings to create a new G Suite account using the domain name provided by your instructor.
   a) Go to **https://gsuite.google.com/signup/basic/business**.
   b) Select **Next**.
   c) In the **Tell us about your business** section, in the **Business or organization name** field, enter *Building with Heart*
   d) In the **Number of employees** field, use the spinner control to select **2-9 employees**.
   e) In the **About you** section, complete the **Name** fields with a First and Last name.
   f) In the **Email** field, enter *admin@<your_domain.com>* replacing <your_domain.com> with your assigned domain name.
   g) In the **Phone number** field, enter a phone number with a valid area code.

   Note: You can avoid entering a working phone number by entering a valid area code and an imaginary number.

   h) Select **Next**.

2. Enter your Business Domain Address.
   a) Select the **Yes, I have one I can use** button.
   b) In the **Your own domain** field, enter the domain name provided by your instructor.
   c) Select **Next**.
   d) At the **Use this domain to set up the account?** prompt, select **Next**.

3. On the **Create your G Suite Account** page, enter your admin email address.
   a) In the **What's your name?** field, enter *admin* as the user name for the G Suite admin email address.
   b) In the **Create password** field, enter the password provided by your instructor.
   c) In the **Secondary email address** field, enter a functional email address that you can access.
   d) In the **reCAPTCHA** field, check **I am not a robot**.
   e) Select the **Accept and Create Account** button.
   f) Select **GO TO SETUP**.

g) Select **NEXT** to use the self-guided setup process.

4. **Follow the prompts to sign in to the Admin console as the admin.**
   a) Verify that the admin email address is correct and enter the admin password and then select **NEXT**.
   b) If asked to save the password with Google Smart Lock, select **NEVER**.
   c) Select **Accept**.

5. **Verify your email address.**
   a) Select **Verify** to send an email to the admin.
   b) Select **Click here** to continue.
      You are presented with two options for setting up the domain—call a Google Advisor or work through the setup on your own.

How would you like to set up your account?

Set up with a Google Advisor	Set up on your own
Call us and we'll walk you through the steps	Experts only
1-844-420-0597	• I'm comfortable managing DNS settings • I have no questions about G Suite • I've administered similar services before
Temporary PIN: 91157178	Self-guided activation
	NEXT

c) Select **NEXT** to select the self-guided activation option and see the set-up options shown here.

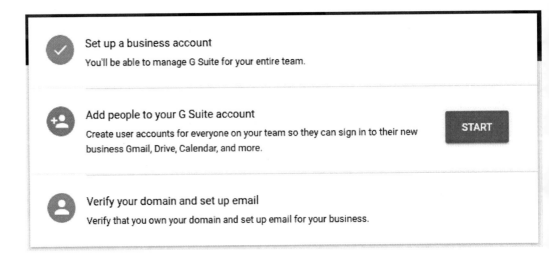

6. Follow the prompts to add one user account and notify them that their email has been moved to Gmail.
   a) Select **START**.
   b) In the **First name** field, enter *Student* and in the **Last name** field, enter *01* for your new user account.
   c) In the **Username** field, enter *student01*
   d) Select **ADD**.
      Student 01 is now listed with (You) admin@<your_domain.com>.
   e) Select **I added all user email addresses currently using @<your_domain.com>**.
   f) Select **NEXT** to move past adding users.
   g) On the **Notify your team** page, enter your admin email address *admin@<your_domain.com>*
   h) Select the **SEND EMAILS** button.
      A welcome email will be sent to this user's Gmail.

7. Verify your ownership of the domain.
   a) In the **Verify your domain and set up email** section, observe the message at the bottom about getting help.

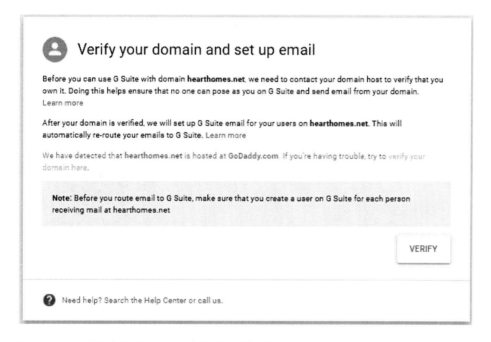

   You can use the Help Center or call a Google advisor.
   b) Select the **VERIFY** button.

c) Follow your instructor's directions to verify your domain. Refresh your browser window and compare your screen to the following image.

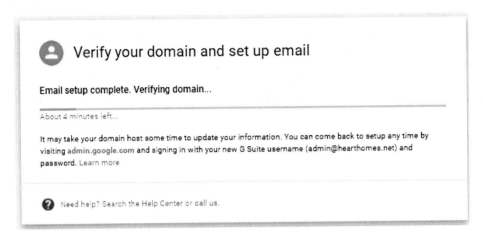

The verification process might take a few minutes, depending on the domain host.

d) Observe the following verified complete message.

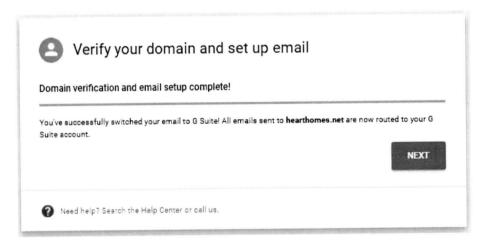

e) Select **NEXT** to advance to the **Pick the right plan for your business** screen.
f) In the **G Suite Business** section, select **CHOOSE**.
The Admin console is displayed.

TOPIC B

Navigate the Admin Console

For administrators, the Admin console provides a control-center dashboard containing links to your domain users and apps, useful tools, and common tasks. From here, you have access to the configuration pages that are used to create, manage, monitor, and maintain your domain.

Admin Console

You can use the *Admin console* to manage your user accounts, company profile, services, applications, and settings for your G Suite account. The main screen, called the Admin console dashboard, contains controls for performing domain management tasks, such as creating user accounts, configuring storage settings, and managing apps. Anyone with administrator privileges can access it by navigating to ***admin.google.com*** and logging in with your Google account credentials. Once logged in, you can select the **Admin** icon from the Google apps icon grid to open the Admin console.

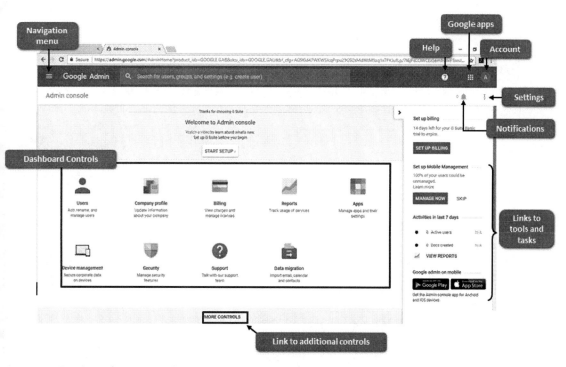

Figure 1-2: The Admin console.

You will find additional controls for managing Groups, Admin roles, Domains, and App Engine apps in the **MORE CONTROLS** section at the bottom of the screen. You can drag the frequently used controls to the dashboard so they are readily available.

Figure 1-3: More Controls in the Admin console.

G Suite Administrative APIs

Many administrative tasks can also be performed through the G Suite Administrative APIs, which enable programmers to write scripts and applications to automate tasks. Administrative tasks that can be automated in the Admin APIs include migrating email and groups over from other IT infrastructures, creating users, and auditing user activity. Super Admins have access to all Admin APIs; however, some of the APIs will need to be enabled by using the Admin console.

 Note: Google periodically updates the layout of its Admin console. Be aware that some documentation you will find on the Internet on how to perform certain tasks in the Admin console may be outdated.

Custom Logo Requirements

You can customize the Admin console by adding your company logo to it. Additionally, the company logo will be visible to all users and in all products in your domain. The logo image dimension and size requirements are as follows:

- Image must be in PNG or GIF format.
- Maximum dimensions are 320 × 132 pixels.
- Maximum size is 30 KB.
- No Google trademarks are allowed.

G Suite Editions

There are a variety of editions available to G Suite users: G Suite Basic, G Suite Business, G Suite Enterprise, and G Suite for Education, Nonprofits, or Government. All editions include the suite of business apps for messaging, storage, web forums, and other services. The full suite of apps includes Gmail™, Google Calendar™, Contacts, Google Drive™, Google Docs™, Hangouts™, Google Groups™ for Business, Blogger™, and YouTube™.

Google Vault enables an organization to retain, archive, search, export, and provide audit reports on the organization's email documents. This app might be useful when dealing with compliance standards and policies. Google Vault can be purchased separately in the G Suite Basic edition; however, it is included in the G Suite Business and G Suite for Education editions.

 Note: To learn more about how to record keeping in the cloud, check out the LearnTO **Use Google Vault** presentation from the **LearnTO** tile on the CHOICE Course screen.

All editions allow an unlimited number of users; however, the storage capacity per user is different. In G Suite Basic, each user has 30 GB for email, document, and image storage. In G Suite Business and G Suite Business Enterprise, each user has unlimited storage.

 Note: As of December 6, 2012, the free edition of Google Apps for new users is no longer available. If you are currently using the legacy free edition, you can continue to use it or upgrade to G Suite Basic or G Suite Business.

	G Suite Basic	G Suite Business/G Suite for Education	G Suite Enterprise
Business Apps	Messaging: Gmail, Calendar, Contacts	All G Suite Basic apps and services	All G Suite Business apps and services
	Storage and collaboration: Drive, Docs, Hangouts	Domain-wide mail and document search, email retention: Vault	Advanced mobile device management features
	Web forums and shared inboxes: Groups for Business	Unified search and assist for content in G Suite services: Cloud Search	Advanced controls and features, such as DLP and S/MIME encryption
	Other Google services: Blogger, YouTube, and more		
	Vault: Available as a paid add-on		
Maximum Number of Users	Unlimited	Unlimited	Unlimited
Storage	30 GB per user	Unlimited storage (1 TB per user for fewer than five users)	Unlimited storage (1 TB per user for fewer than five users)
Support	24/7 phone and email support	24/7 phone and email support	24/7 phone and email support

For additional comparison details, you can check out the online G Suite Administrator Help document **Compare G Suite editions** at **https://support.google.com**.

G Suite Apps and Services

You can use the Admin console to control the apps and services in your G Suite domain. Google has a tendency to refer to apps and services interchangeably. Use the **Apps** icon to access and manage the G Suite apps and additional Google services. From a user's perspective, you are probably familiar with Gmail, Calendar, Contacts, Drive, and Hangouts. As the administrator, you now have access to additional Google services such as Groups for Business, Google AdWords™, and Google Analytics™.

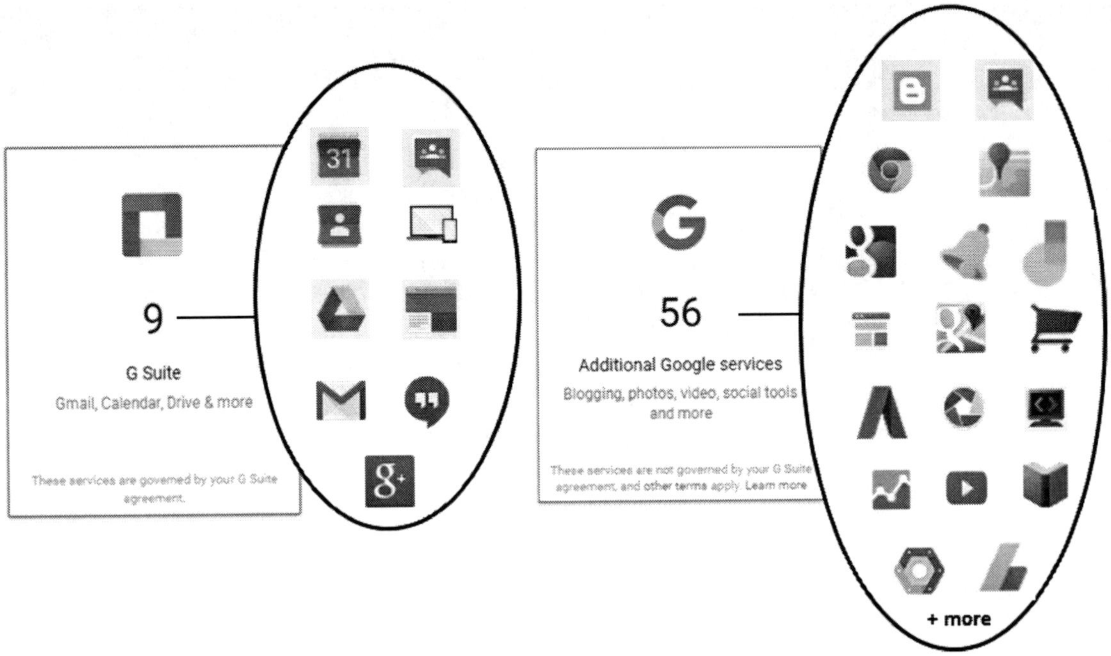

Figure 1-4: G Suite Apps and Services.

Note: If your business is education, such as running a school or university, you will have a few more education apps and features available to you.

G Suite Status Dashboard

You can view the service status by selecting the **G Suite Status Dashboard** link on the Admin console. G Suite services can be turned on and off for everyone, specific organizational units, or individual users. By default, organizational units inherit the setting of its parent organization. In some cases, this is the top-level domain. When available, you can choose to overwrite the inheritance, if desired.

Access the Checklist tile on your CHOICE Course screen for reference information and job aids on How to Navigate the Admin Console.

ACTIVITY 1-3
Using the Admin Console

Data File
C:\093008Data\Getting Started with G Suite Administration\BWH_logo.png

Before You Begin
Your G Suite domain has been created with you as the admin and one other user named Student 01.

Scenario
As the administrator for the Building with Heart organization, you will need to manage the G Suite domain and make sure your users can communicate and collaborate. To familiarize yourself with the features of this tool, you'll examine in the Admin console and then use it to customize your Company profile.

1. Observe the Admin console dashboard controls.
    a) In the upper-right corner of the screen, verify that you are signed in as the admin.

     Note: You can always access the Admin console by typing **admin.google.com** in the **Address** bar of the Chrome browser.

    b) Observe the Admin console dashboard controls in the middle of the screen.

    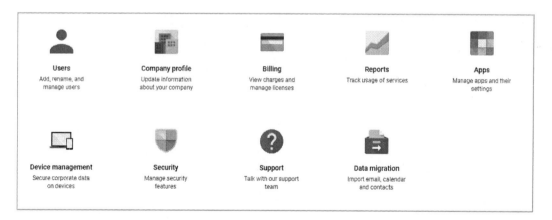

    These controls are used to open pages that contain settings for managing your domain as indicated by the description below each icon. For example, you select **Users** to manage the user accounts in your domain.

c) In the upper-left corner, select the **Main menu** icon to display the menu of admin controls.

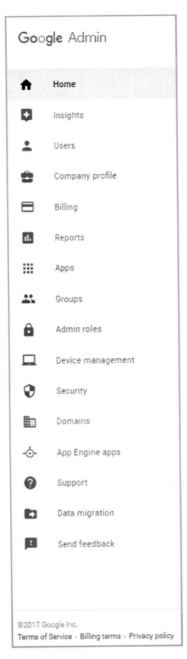

The menu contains the same controls as those found on the Admin console dashboard. You will discover that there are multiple ways to access pages and settings for your G Suite account.

d) Select **Home** to return to the main **Admin console** page.

2. Change the default header logo of the **Company Profile** to the image file **BWH_logo**.

   a) From the Admin console, select **Company profile**.
   The **Company Profile** page contains settings for your company information, communication preferences, and custom logos and URLs.

   b) Select **Personalization** and then select **Custom logo**.

   c) Select **CHOOSE FILE**, navigate to C:\093008Data\Getting Started with G Suite Administration, and double-click to open **BWH_logo**.

d) Select **UPLOAD** to add the company logo to your domain pages.
   e) Check **Show this logo in all sites that users create**.
   f) Select **SAVE**.

3. Return to the **Home** page of the Admin console.
   a) In the upper-left corner of the screen, select the **Google Admin** button to quickly display the Admin console Home page.
   b) In the right pane, observe the billing, tools, and common task information that's displayed below the current user's name.

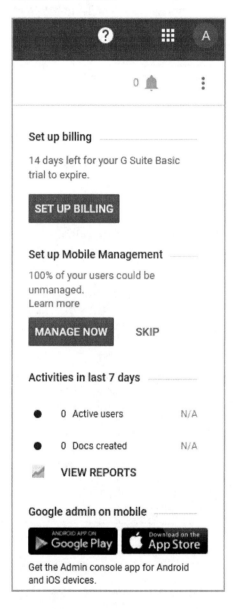

   This area of the Admin console displays activity stats, links to tools and other common tasks, and recommended apps. If you are using a trial version, you will see the number of days left before the trial expires with a button to set up billing.

4. View the Google services running for your domain on the G Suite Status Dashboard.

a) On the right side of the **Home** page, in the **Tools** section, select the **G Suite Status Dashboard** link.

```
Tools
Get help from a partner
G Suite Marketplace
G Suite Status Dashboard
The G Suite Referral Program
Transfer tool for unmanaged users
```

The G Suite Status Dashboard opens on a separate browser tab and displays the performance information for your G Suite services.

b) Navigate to the bottom of the page to view the service indicator legend.

```
All times are shown in your local timezone unless otherwise noted.
  ○ No Issues    ● Service disruption    ○ Service outage
```

The green dots to the left of the Google service indicate that it is functioning with no issues. Because this Google domain is relatively new, you probably won't see any service disruptions or outages.

c) Close the G Suite Status Dashboard browser tab.

5. **Move the Admin roles control to the main part of the dashboard.**

   a) At the bottom of the **Admin console** tab, select **MORE CONTROLS** to display additional icons.

   b) Drag the **Admin roles** control up to the dashboard.

   c) When an outline labeled **Drop here** appears, release the mouse button to move the icon.

   > **Note:** You can also select the plus (+) sign in the upper-right corner of the control to quickly move it to the dashboard.

   d) Observe the notification at the top of the page.

   ```
   Q  Search for users, groups, and settings (e.g. create user)
                              Admin roles has been added to your Admin Console dashboard
   ```

   > **Note:** With the exception of Users, Company Profile, and Billing, you can move the icons between the Admin console dashboard and the More Controls as you wish.

   e) Select **MORE CONTROLS** again to collapse the section.

Summary

In this lesson, you learned about G Suite domains and the importance of planning the domain before setting it up. Then, you created a new G Suite domain and examined the Admin console dashboard that is used to manage the domain.

Have you had experience setting up a new G Suite domain? Any pitfalls?

Is G Suite a desirable business solution for your company? Why or why not?

Note: Check your CHOICE Course screen for opportunities to interact with your classmates, peers, and the larger CHOICE online community about the topics covered in this course or other topics you are interested in. From the Course screen you can also access available resources for a more continuous learning experience.

2 | Managing User Accounts

Lesson Time: 2 hours

Lesson Introduction

A large portion of your job as the administrator will be managing user accounts. After creating the accounts, the next most common request will involve lost and forgotten passwords. But, there are other user management tasks that will require your attention. As users come and go at your organization, you'll need to suspend, delete, and possibly restore, their accounts. To share the administrative burden of the G Suite domain, you can give other users admin privileges so they can help you with administrative tasks.

Lesson Objectives

In this lesson, you will:

- Create and modify user accounts.
- Assign admin roles to user accounts.
- Suspend, restore, and remove user accounts.
- Generate and reset user passwords.

TOPIC A

Create and Modify User Accounts

After setting up your domain, your next administrative task is to create user accounts and manage their settings. You can add users one at a time or as a group. You can even send a user an invitation to create their own user account in your domain.

The Users Page

From the Admin console, you can select the **Users** control to display the list of the user accounts in your domain. The toolbar at the top contains buttons for filtering the user list by type or by organization. You can also access Help and other menu options, such as selecting columns to be displayed, to work with your user list. You can use the **Menu** icon at the right end of the user to perform user-related actions, such as renaming the user or resetting the password.

You can select users from the list by pointing to the user's picture until it changes to a check box. As soon as you select one user, the other users' pictures become check boxes. Use this technique to select and manage multiple users with one command.

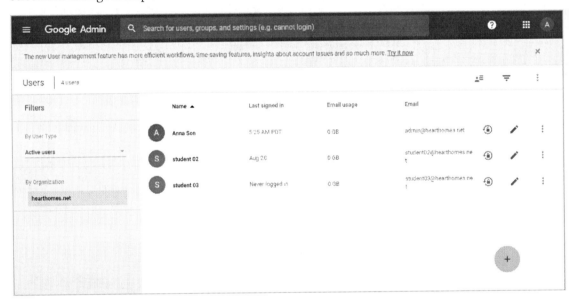

Figure 2-1: The Users page.

New User Accounts

Creating and managing user accounts might consume a large amount of your administrative time. From the **Users** page, you have the option to individually create new user accounts or create multiple users from a CSV spreadsheet file. When you point to the user action button, it expands to include a button for each method of adding a user. Regardless of the option you choose, the following four fields are required for each new user: First name, Last name, Email address, and Password.

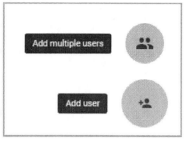

Figure 2-2: Adding user accounts.

For passwords, you can accept the temporary password from Google or set your own temporary password. When you accept the temporary password generated by Google, you can email it to the user so they can log in to their new G Suite account. Either way, the user will be prompted to change their password the first time they sign in to the domain.

When adding multiple users from a file, it's critical that the first four columns of the spreadsheet are First name, Last name, Email Address, and Password. You must save the spreadsheet as a CSV file. Google provides a sample spreadsheet that you can download and modify to ensure that the list of users you want to add is formatted correctly.

 Access the Checklist tile on your CHOICE Course screen for reference information and job aids on How to Create and Modify User Accounts.

ACTIVITY 2-1
Creating User Accounts

Before You Begin
As the creator of the domain, you are the Super Admin.

Scenario
Your organization, Building with Heart, is experiencing a growth spurt and needs to add user accounts to your domain.

1. From the Admin console, create a new user account.
   a) Sign in with your admin credentials, if you are not already signed in.
   b) Select **Users** to access the **Users** page.

   > Note: The **Filters** pane on the left can be shown or hidden by selecting the **Filters** button on the toolbar at the top of the screen.

   By default, the **Users** page displays the Active users.

   c) In the lower-right corner of the screen, point to the **Add** button.
      The single **Add user** button expands to include an additional button to **Add multiple users**.
   d) When the button focus changes, select the **Add user** button.

   e) In the **Create a new user** dialog box, in the **First name** field, type *Student*
   f) In the **Last name** field, type *02*
   g) In the **Primary email address** field, type *student02* using the same number as the previous step.

   h) Accept the auto-generated temporary password and select **CREATE**.

Note: You can specify a temporary password by selecting **Set Password**.

2. Send an email with sign-in instructions to the owner of the new user account.
   a) In the **Create a new user** dialog box, select **Show password** to view the auto-generated password.

   b) Select **SEND EMAIL** to mail the sign-in instructions.
      An email containing the user name and temporary password appears.
   c) In the **To** field, enter *Student02@<your_domain.com>*

 Note: Normally, you would enter an email address that the user has access to, such as a Gmail address. However, for the purposes of class, you'll use the *@<your_domain.com>* address.

   d) At the bottom of the screen, select **SEND**.
   e) Observe the new user account on the **Users** page.

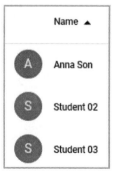

3. Display email addresses on the **Users** page.

a) In the upper-right corner of the window, select the **Menu** icon.

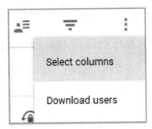

b) Select **Select columns**.
c) In the **Select columns** dialog box, select **Email address** to add email addresses to the **Users** page display.
d) Select **APPLY**.
   A new **Email** column appears immediately on the **Users** page.

TOPIC B

Use System Roles to Delegate Duties to Users

It's recommended that organizations have at least two administrators who have full control of the Google account. Assigning administrative privileges to others provides backup support to the top admin and enables them to delegate some specific functions and related tasks, such as managing users or groups. However, you need to be judicious when delegating admin privileges because having too many admins can pose a risk too.

User Profile

Selecting a user from the **Users** page opens a **User Profile** page containing all of the account details, including the date and time of their last login, the documents they own and the amount of mail storage they've used. Additional links contain configuration settings, such as enabled G Suite apps, groups, license, security, roles and privileges, devices, and enabled services. The toolbar at the top of the profile contains user-related action buttons that can be used to modify the user's settings and manage the user account. By default, the user profile appears as shown in the following figure. You can select **Show more** to see additional settings.

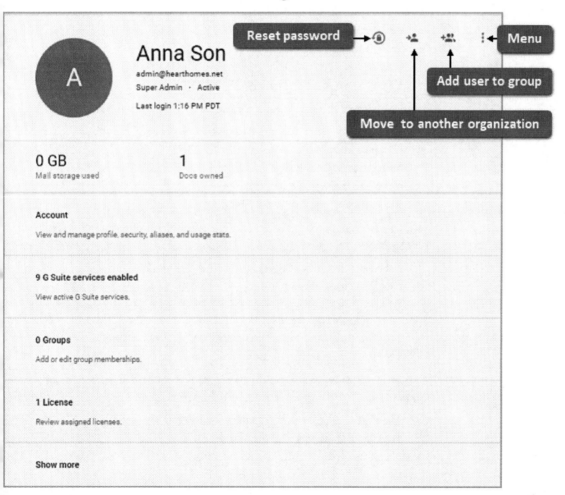

Figure 2-3: The User Profile page.

Types of Administrator Roles

There are six pre-defined administrator roles that can be assigned to users to assist in the management of the G Suite account. The names are relatively self-explanatory with the Super Admin having access and control of everything in the G Suite account domain. As the creator of the domain, you are a Super Admin for your domain. To provide backup and share the workload, it's recommended that an organization have at least two administrators with Super Admin privileges.

There are two different approaches when assigning admin roles to users. You can open the **User** page and assign an admin role or specific privileges to the user. The second method is to open the **Admin Roles** page and assign, or remove, specific users to the role. If the pre-defined system roles do not meet your needs, you can create a custom role.

The following table describes the pre-defined system roles for G Suite administrators. You can also create custom roles if these pre-defined roles do not meet your needs.

Administrator Role	Privileges
Super Admin *Note: The domain creator is a Super Admin.*	Full access to everything in the Admin console and Admin API and ability to manage the entire G Suite domain. Only Super Admins have the ability to: • Set up billing • Create and assign admin roles • Modify the admin's settings, including reset admin passwords • Restore deleted users • Perform email log searches • Create, modify, and delete sub organizations • View users' calendars and event details
Groups Admin	Full access to Google Groups created in the Admin console, including: • View user profiles and organization structure • Create and delete groups • Manage group membership • Manage group access settings • Read access to sub organizations
User Management Admin	Full access to manage user accounts, excluding administrators. Privileges include: • View user profiles and organizational structure • Read access to sub organizations • Create, rename, and delete user accounts • Change user passwords • Manage user's individual password and security settings • Grant specific rights to individual users
Help Desk Admin	Limited access to organization structure and user profiles. Privileges include: • View user profiles and organizational structure • Read access to sub organizations • Reset user passwords, excluding administrators

Administrator Role	Privileges
Services Admin	Full access to manage products, services, and devices that have been added to the domain. Using the Admin console, this includes: • Turn services on or off • Modify service settings and permissions • Customize service addresses • Manage Chrome and mobile devices • Read access to sub organizations
Reseller Admin	The ability to provision and manage your customers using the G Suite account. The Reseller Admin does not use the Admin console, but can: • Access the Reseller console to manage customers and their subscriptions • Access the Admin consoles of customers' domains • Use reseller-related APIs

Access the Checklist tile on your CHOICE Course screen for reference information and job aids on How to Assign Admin Roles.

ACTIVITY 2-2
Assigning Admin Roles to Users

Before You Begin
Your domain has two accounts: you as the Super Admin and two regular users (Student 01 and Student 02).

Scenario
Currently, you are the only Super Admin for your Google domain. Before you can create and manage user accounts, you need to have the proper administrative privileges. Additionally, granting the Super Admin role to others will provide a backup in case of emergencies.

1. Assign the Super Admin role to the new Student 02 account.
   a) From the **Users** page, open the user profile for **Student 02**.
   b) Scroll to the bottom of the page and select **Show more**.
   c) Select **Admin roles and privileges** to expand the settings.
   d) Select **MANAGE ROLES**.
   e) In the **Manage roles** dialog box, select **Super Admin**.

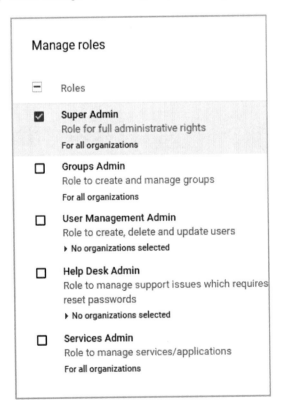

f) Select **UPDATE ROLES**.
    A message that the roles have been successfully added should appear.

    Roles successfully added to the selected user.

2. **Sign in as Student 02 to verify that the Super Admin rights have been assigned.**
    a) From the **Account** menu, select **Sign out** to sign out from the Admin account.
    b) At the Google account sign-in page, sign in as *student02@<your_domain.com>* using your domain name.
    c) When prompted, enter Student 02's temporary password.
    d) Change and confirm your password.

     Note: By default, users are required to change their password after they first sign in.

    e) From the Admin console **Home** page, select **Users→Student 02** to open the user profile.
    f) Scroll to the bottom of the page and select **Show more**.
    g) Select **1 Admin roles and privileges** and verify that you have been granted the Super Admin role.

    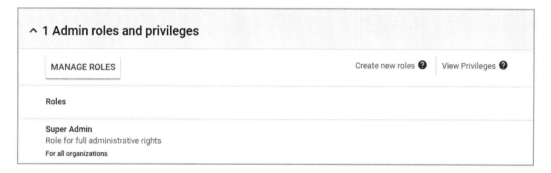

3. **From the Users page, add a new user account with an email address of student03@<your_domain.com>.**
    a) In the upper-left corner of the screen, select **Users** to return to the **Users** page.
    b) On the **Users** page, select **Add user**.
    c) In the **First name** field, type *Student* and in the **Last name** field, type *03*
    d) In the **Primary email address** field, type *student03*
    e) Select **Set Password** and enter the temporary password for this user and record it on your Domain worksheet.
    f) Select **CREATE**.
        You might see a message about protecting against spammers and abuse. It basically states that Student 03 will need a passcode the first time that user logs in. Google sends the verification passcode to a phone number either by voice or text message.
    g) Select **SEND EMAIL**, and enter an email address.
    h) Select **SEND**.
        Student 03 appears in the Users list. However, if the passcode message was displayed, then Student 03 will not appear in the Users list until they sign in and verify their identity using the passcode sent from Google.

ACTIVITY 2-3
Enabling Multiple Sign-In

Before You Begin

You are currently signed in as Student 02 (Super Admin).

Scenario

As the administrator, you want to use your Admin account for admin-related tasks and use the Student 01 account when exchanging email with others, especially those outside of your domain. This can help you distinguish between your separate roles—as the admin and as a regular user. You'll also want to be able to sign in so you can verify that the new configuration settings for domain users hold true.

1. Sign out as Student 02 and sign in as Admin.
    a) Select the **Account** menu that displays Student 02 and select **Sign out**.
    b) In the **Email** field, type *Admin@<your_domain.com>* and the password.
    c) If available, uncheck **Stay signed in** and then select **Sign in**.

2. While signed in as the Admin, add a second account to the account menu.
    a) Select the **Google apps** icon and then select the **Gmail** icon to open **Gmail** on a separate tab.
    b) From your account name, display your **Account** menu.

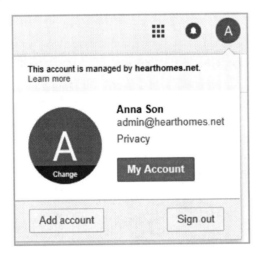

   c) Select **Add account**.
   d) In the **Email** field, type *student01@<your_domain.com>* and select **Next**.
   e) In the **Password** field, type the user's password and select **Sign in**.
   f) When prompted, select **I accept. Continue to my account.** and change your password.
      You are now signed in as Student 01 and that user's Gmail appears on a separate tab.

3. Use the **Account** menu to switch between signed-in accounts.

a) From the account name, display your **Account** menu.

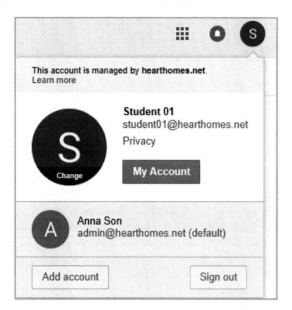

b) Select **admin@<your_domain.com>** to switch to your Admin account without signing out of the current account.
   This multiple sign-in method enables you to smoothly switch between the Admin and Student 03 accounts. However, each time you switch between accounts, a new browser tab is opened.
c) Close all of the open Gmail tabs.

TOPIC C

Remove and Restore User Accounts

As users leave your company, you will need to remove the user accounts. However, if an employee is just taking a temporary leave of absence, you can suspend the account to make it inactive. Then, depending on whether the employee returns or not, you can reactivate or restore the account or delete it.

User Account Suspension

For employees who are going on a sabbatical or taking a temporary leave of absence, you can suspend their user account and deactivate it. They will no longer be able to sign in to the domain and access services, such as Gmail, Drive, and Calendar. They will also be unable to receive invitations sent through Gmail or Calendar. Any data that the user owns will remain, but you might want to transfer its ownership before suspending the account. You will not be prompted to transfer data ownership when you're suspending the user. The disadvantage to suspending a user is that the account continues to use a user license.

 Note: Another business case for suspending an account might be after an employee has been terminated and it has not yet been decided what to do with their archival mail.

You can restore suspended users from the user profile and return them to active status.

Figure 2-4: Suspending an account.

User Account Removal

When it becomes necessary to delete an account, the actual process of doing so is relatively simple. You can delete user accounts individually or as a group from the **Users** page in the Admin console. When you delete an account, the user's mail, calendar data, Drive files, and YouTube videos are deleted after five days. Any site pages that the user created will not be deleted, but can be removed by an administrator.

Before deleting an account, you need to transfer the ownership of their Drive documents to avoid losing important data. Additionally, you will need to transfer ownership of any shared calendars that the user owns and manages. Transferring ownership isn't restricted to the **User Deletion** dialog box, but it's usually thought about at this time.

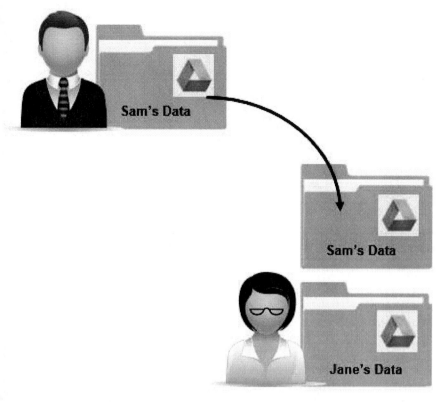

Figure 2-5: Transferring ownership of data.

When you delete an account, the user license becomes available for another user. Maintaining the appropriate number of user accounts is an important part of managing the total bill for your Google account. When the deletion is complete, the domain's primary and secondary admin contacts will receive a confirmation email.

 Access the Checklist tile on your **CHOICE** Course screen for reference information and job aids on **How to Remove a User Account**.

ACTIVITY 2-4
Suspending a User Account

Before You Begin
In addition to your Admin account, you have three user accounts. Student 02 is a Super Admin. Student 01 and Student 03 are users.

Scenario
Due to the nature of home building, the Building with Heart organization employs some seasonal crews that work only during the peak season. Some user accounts can be temporarily suspended to limit the amount of traffic and activity in the domain.

1. Open the user profile for **Student 03**.
    a) At the Admin console, select **Users**.
    b) Select *Student 03* to open the user profile.
    By opening the user profile, you can see the total number of documents that the user owns.

    > **Note:** Because a suspended user will not be able to access the files that they own, it's recommended that they transfer ownership of the files. If they haven't done so, you as the Admin can transfer the file ownership before suspending the user account.

2. Suspend the user account.
    a) Select the **Menu** icon and then select **Suspend**.

    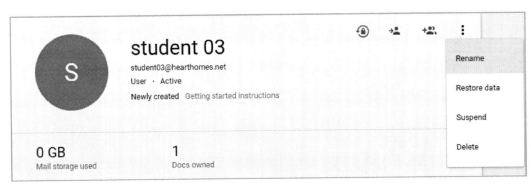

    The **Suspend Student 03** dialog box appears and explains what suspending the account means. As shown in red text, suspended users still require a user license.
    b) Select **SUSPEND USER**.
    The text "Suspended" appears to the right of the user name at the top of the profile.
    c) Verify that Student 03 has been suspended by navigating back to the **Users** page.
    The suspended user does not appear on the main **Users** page because it's currently displaying Active users.

User Account Restoration

You have up to five days to restore a deleted account. After five days, you will be unable to recover the deleted account's mail, calendar data, and Drive files. However, there are no guarantees that the data will be fully recovered, so it's important that you transfer ownership before deleting an account. It might take two hours for the account to be fully restored. Some circumstances will prevent you from restoring a user account:

- If a matching group, user name, or email alias was created after the user account was deleted, then a "username already exists" error message is displayed.
- If you've exceeded your available user licenses, then a "domain is over user limit" message is displayed.

 Access the Checklist tile on your CHOICE Course screen for reference information and job aids on **How to Restore a User Account.**

ACTIVITY 2-5
Restoring a User Account

Before You Begin
The user account for Student 03 has been suspended.

Scenario
As the new building season ramps up again, you need to restore the user accounts that have been dormant for the past few months.

1. In the **Filters** pane, view the suspended users.
   a) From the **By User Type** list, observe that **Active users** are displayed in the **Users** page.
   b) Select the **By User Type** drop-down arrow to expand the menu. You can control which users are displayed in the **Users** page based on different user types.
   c) Select **Suspended users** to display the recently suspended user accounts.

2. Restore the suspended **Student 03** account.
   a) From the **Users** page, select the suspended user to open the user profile.

   While you can suspend a user account from the **Users** page, you must open the individual user profile to restore the account.

   b) Select the **Menu** icon and select **Restore user** to instantly restore the user account.

3. Verify that the Student 03 account is active again.

a) Observe the user profile heading.

b) Return to the **Users** page and notice that **Student 03** has been restored to the **Active users** list.

TOPIC D

Manage User Passwords

A large portion of the administrative requests from users will be about passwords. You can reset a forgotten password or you can force a user to change the password themselves. Forcing users to change their own passwords is useful when you suspect that the password was compromised. You don't want to risk compromising the entire domain by waiting for the user.

Reset Passwords

To share the administrative workload, you can delegate password-related tasks to another user by giving them User Management Admin privileges. While this can reduce the amount of password requests that come to you, keep in mind that only a Super Admin can reset an administrator's passwords. From the Admin console **Users** page, you can access the **Reset password** icon for individual users. When resetting the password, you have the option to create a password or have Google automatically generate a password. Regardless of the method you choose to obtain a new password, you should require the user to change the password the next time they sign in to their Google account.

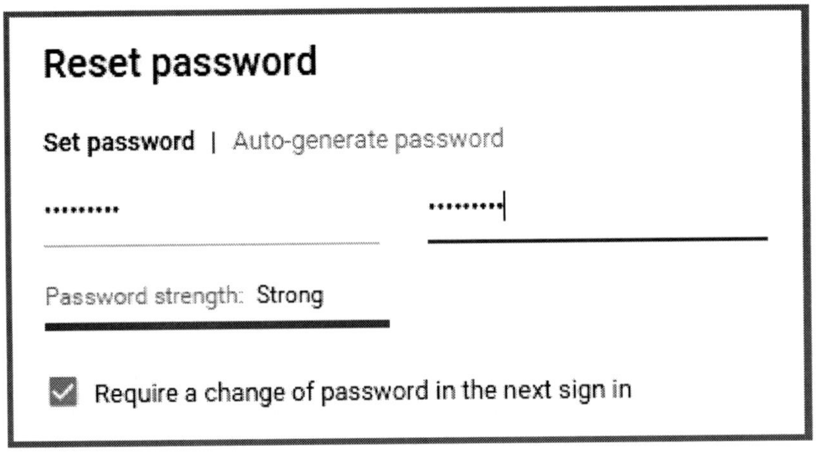

Figure 2-6: Resetting a user's password.

From the **User Profile** page, in the **Account** settings, you can force the user to change their password the next time they sign in. In the case of a lost or stolen device, you can immediately disrupt the connection and force a password change. You can use the **Reset sign-in cookies** link and force the user to sign in again if they want to continue to access their G Suite account.

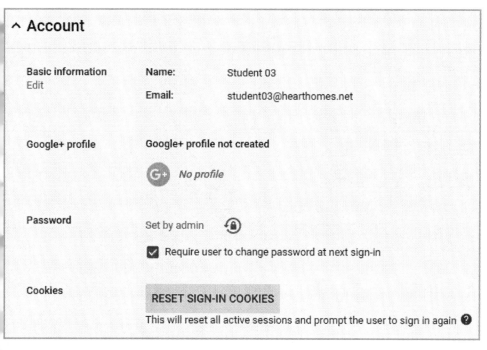

Figure 2-7: Resetting sign-in cookies.

Guidelines for Creating Strong Passwords

 Note: All of the Guidelines for this lesson are available as checklists from the **Checklist** tile on the CHOICE Course screen.

Use the following guidelines to create strong user passwords.

Create Strong Passwords

To create strong user passwords:

- Set minimum length to 8 characters (longer than 10 for strong passwords).
- Include special characters, such as @ * > and so on.
- Include numbers.
- Use a combination of uppercase and lowercase letters.
- Replace similar sounding words for abbreviations or your own creative spellings.
- Avoid using easy-to-discover passwords, such as pet names, identifying personal information, words found in the dictionary, repeating characters, and keyboard patterns or sequential numbers.
- Avoid reusing your passwords.

Automatic Password Generation

If you choose to have Google automatically generate a random password, you have the option to notify the user of their new temporary password by email. However, if they are having trouble signing on, then emailing their new password is only useful if they've provided a secondary recovery email address. You can select **Show password** to view the auto-generated password.

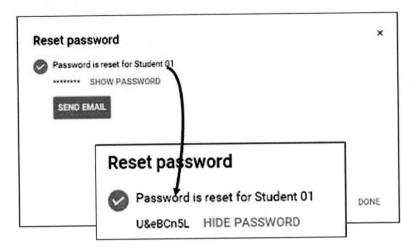

Figure 2-8: Automatic password generation.

ACTIVITY 2-6
Resetting a User Password

Scenario

You've created a user account and before the user could sign in for the first time, they've forgotten their temporary password. You've received a request from Student 01 to reset their password.

1. As the Administrator, reset the password for Student01@*<your_domain.com>*.
    a) If necessary, display the **Users** page.
    b) Select **Student 01** and select the **Reset password** icon.
    c) In the **Reset password** dialog box, select **Auto-generate password** to allow Google to create the new temporary password.
    d) Check **Require a change of password in the next sign in**.
    e) Select **RESET**.
    f) Select **SHOW PASSWORD** to display the auto-generated password.
    g) Record the password or copy it to your clipboard.
    h) Select **DONE**.

2. As Student01@*<your_domain.com>*, verify that your password has been reset.
    a) From the **Account** menu, sign out as the Admin so you can sign in as **Student 01**.
    b) On the Google **Choose an Account** page, select **Add account**.
    c) In the **Email** field, enter *Student01@<your_domain.com>* and select **NEXT**.
    d) In the **Password** field, enter the temporary password from the previous step and select **NEXT**.
    e) Select **Accept**.
    f) When prompted to change the password, type a new password and confirm it. Then, select **Change password**.

3. As a user, if you're unable to sign in to your Google account, what help is available to you?

Password Management

You can use the **Admin console→Security** page to configure the minimum and maximum password lengths requirement for all users in your domain. Increasing the minimum required length has the potential to increase security by forcing users to create longer passwords. Even though Google prevents users from saving weak passwords, ultimately the passwords are only as strong as users make them. Once a password is hacked, the intruder now has access to the user's contact list, as well as the ability to send mail on behalf of the compromised user account.

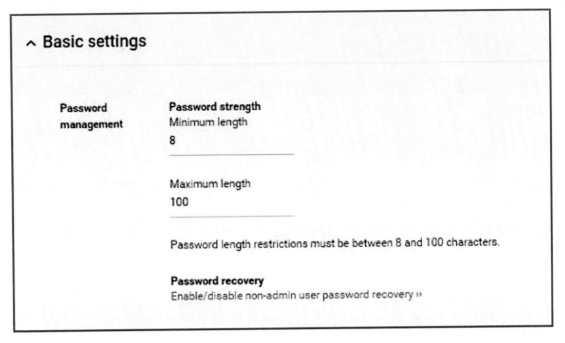

Figure 2-9: Basic security settings.

In the **Password monitoring** section, you can see a list of users in your domain, the length of their individual passwords, and the password strength. This enables you to identify the weaker, or potentially vulnerable, passwords. You can select the user name to open the **User Profile** page and take the necessary action.

In the **Password Strength** column, the following colors are used to indicate password strength:

- Green for Strong
- Blue for Good
- Yellow for Weak
- Gray for Poor

 Access the Checklist tile on your CHOICE Course screen for reference information and job aids on How to Manage User Passwords.

ACTIVITY 2-7
Monitoring and Configuring Password Settings

Before You Begin
Student 03 has been suspended.

Scenario
As the administrator, it's good practice to periodically monitor the user passwords in your domain. Upon doing so, you see that Student 03, your suspended user, has a weak password. You want to force Student 03 to change their password and make it stronger. To encourage a stronger password, you'll change the minimum length.

---

1. View the strength of your domain users' passwords.
    a) Verify that you are signed in as the Admin.
    b) From the Admin console, select **Security**.
    c) Select **Password monitoring** to expand the settings.

NAME	PASSWORD LENGTH	PASSWORD STRENGTH
Anna Son	9	
Student 01	9	
Student 02	9	
Student 03	9	
Student 04	9	

    Each user's password information (length and strength) is displayed. You can easily identify those users who have weak and potentially vulnerable passwords. The password strength criteria is known only to Google and not published.

2. On the **User profile** page, force **Student 03** to change their password.
    a) From the **Password monitoring** list, select **Student 03** to display the profile page.
    b) Select **Account** to expand the settings.

c) In the **Password** settings, check **Require user to change password at next sign-in**.

d) Select **SAVE**.

3. **Verify the forced password change for Student 03.**
   a) Sign in as *Student03@<your_domain.com>*
   b) Enter the current password.
   c) When prompted, type a new password and confirm it.

Password Recovery

On the **Users profile** page, you can specify a recovery phone number or recovery email that enables users to reset their own passwords without assistance from the administrator. When a user forgets their password, at the Google sign-in page, they can select the **Forgot password?** link. The password recovery wizard guides them through the steps to have a recovery code sent as a text message to a phone number that they can use to access their G Suite account.

 Note: This feature is unavailable for domains running Single Sign-On (SSO) or G Suite Password Sync (GSPS).

As the Admin, you can use the **Admin console→Security** page to enable the Password Recovery feature for your non-admin users. In the **Basic settings** section, when you select the **Enable/disable non-admin user password recovery** link, it redirects you to the **Advanced security settings** page. The feature is disabled by default.

At any time, you can remove a user's recovery email address and the recovery phone number so they no longer have access to the G Suite domain. This is especially important when employees are terminated or leave the organization.

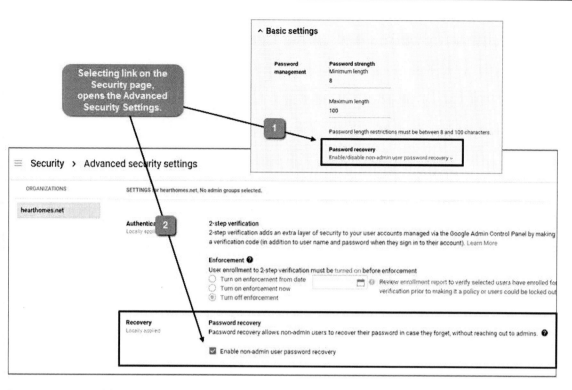

Figure 2-10: Enabling password recovery.

Admin Password Reset

As the Admin, you can reset your password by using the same password recovery method that you've enabled for your users. On your **Account settings** page, you must specify a recovery email, a recovery phone number, or both. Then, when you experience trouble signing in to your Google account, you can select **Need help?** and walk through the steps to reset your password.

For G Suite accounts with more than three Super Admins or 500 users, you are not allowed to reset your admin password in this way. You must have another Admin reset your password by using the Admin console. Another option for resetting your admin password yourself is through your domain host's DNS settings. If you have access, then you can add a CNAME record that contains a 22-character string that begins with "google" to reset the administrator password. By using this method, you might need to wait up to 72 hours before your password has been reset.

 Access the Checklist tile on your CHOICE Course screen for reference information and job aids on How to Recover Passwords.

ACTIVITY 2-8
Enabling Password Recovery for Users

Before You Begin
You will need a separate non-domain address to use as a recovery email.

Scenario
As the administrator, a sizeable portion of your day is spent handling forgotten password requests from users. You can help users be a bit more self-sufficient by giving them the ability to reset their own passwords. In order for this to work, users will need to have an alternative email address, such as a personal Gmail address, which they can use.

1. Configure the Recovery email setting for Student 02.
   a) Use the **Account** menu to sign in as **Student 02**.
   b) From the **Account** menu, select **My Account** to open your **Account** settings on a new tab.
   c) In the **Sign-in & security** section, select the **Signing in to Google** link.
   d) Select **Recovery email** and enter an email address different from your Google account domain address.
   e) Enter your G Suite password.
   f) Select the back arrow to the left of Recovery email.

   g) Close the **Sign-in & security** tab.

2. Sign in as the Admin and enable password recovery help for users.
   a) Sign in as *Admin@<your_domain.com>*
   b) From the Admin console, select **Security→Basic settings**.
   c) In the **Password management** section, under **Password recovery**, select **Enable/disable non-admin user password recovery** to open the **Advanced security settings** page.
   d) In the **Recovery** section, check **Enable non-admin user password recovery**.
   e) Select **SAVE**.

3. Sign in as Student 02 to test the password recovery feature.
   a) From the **Account** menu, sign out from the Admin account.
   b) On the Google sign-in page, select or type *student02@<your_domain.com>*
   c) Select **Forgot password?** to start the password recovery wizard.
      The **Account help** for *<user@your_domain.com>* page is displayed.
   d) In the **Enter the last password you remember** field, choose either of the following options:
      - Enter the most recent password you can recall and select **Next**, or
      - Select **Try a different question**.

e) Observe the message asking you to confirm your recovery email address.

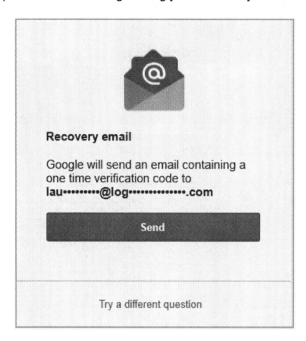

f) Select **Send** to confirm your recovery email address and send a six-digit code to this email address.

4. Sign in to your recovery email account to view the password reset instructions that were sent from Google.
   a) From the **Account** menu, sign out as the current user and sign in with your recovery email address.
   b) Open the email from **Google** to view the instructions.

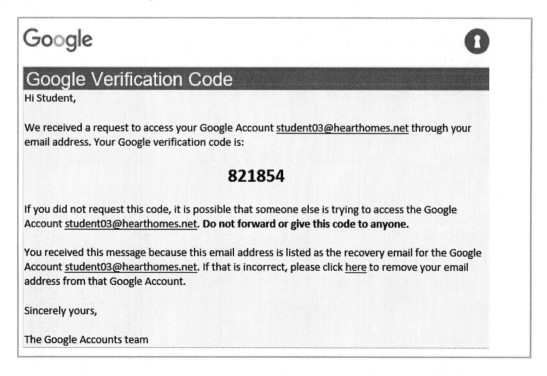

c) As instructed, on the Google sign in page, enter the six-digit code on the Google sign in page to initiate the password reset process.
The **Change password** page appears.

d) Enter and confirm a new password and then select **Change password**.
When successful, the following message appears.

You're now signed in

To help you easily get back into your account if this happens again, take a minute to review your security settings.

Complete your recovery information

Help us get in touch with you if there's unusual activity in your account or you accidentally get locked out. For your security, you may need to re-enter your password to edit recovery information.

        Recovery phone   Add recovery phone

        Recovery email   jgreene82817@gmail.com   Edit

DONE   SKIP

Check your Gmail settings

5. Close all windows and exit the browser.

Summary

In this lesson, you learned that the bulk of an administrator's responsibility is managing users. You created, suspended, restored, and deleted user accounts. To delegate some of your administrative duties, you assigned admin rights to other users. Finally, you helped users recover a lost password by resetting the password at the Admin console dashboard, as well as enabling password recovery so users can be self-sufficient.

What are the advantages of sharing administrative duties between multiple admins?

What are the potential pitfalls to enabling non-admin user password recovery?

> **Note:** Check your CHOICE Course screen for opportunities to interact with your classmates, peers, and the larger CHOICE online community about the topics covered in this course or other topics you are interested in. From the Course screen you can also access available resources for a more continuous learning experience.

3 Using Organizational Units

Lesson Time: 1 hour, 30 minutes

Lesson Introduction

Now that you've created user accounts, you can create organizational units to group users by department or function. Organizational units enable you to collectively manage users who need access to the same services and resources.

Lesson Objectives

In this lesson, you will:

- Create an organizational unit.
- Use organizational units to manage apps and services.

TOPIC A

Create Organizational Units

Organizational units, or sub organizations, are often thought of as children of the top-level, or parent organization. Continuing with the analogy, the children inherit the access policies of the parent organization. You can override these inherited settings, if necessary.

Organizational Structure

Each G Suite domain starts with one top-level organization. As the administrator, you can create organizational units to manage the users and devices within the larger domain. Creating organizational units isn't a domain requirement but they can be an efficient way to configure and control settings for multiple users.

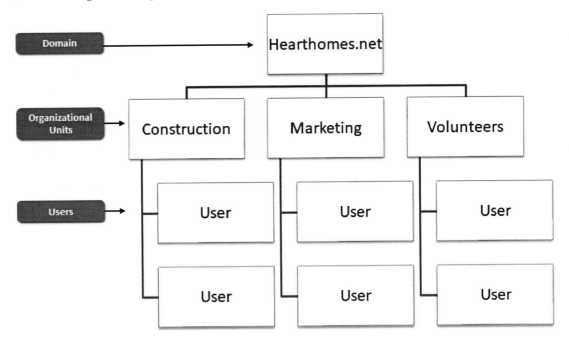

Figure 3-1: Organizational structure of a Google domain.

Organizational Units

In your domain, an *organizational unit* (also called a *sub organization*) can be used to group users and quickly assign rights and privileges to all users in that group. Every domain begins with one top-level organization. You can create as many organizational units as needed. New organizational units are based on their parent organization and will inherit the rights and access to services. The inheritance hierarchy is covered in the next topic.

> **Note:** The terms "sub organizations" and "organizational units" are used interchangeably in this course.

Reasons to Create Organizational Units

Even though organizational units are not required, you might find it beneficial to create organizational units in your domain. Some of the reasons for creating and implementing organizational units are as follows:

- **Delegating Admin Control**: In addition to distributing the administrative workload for the entire organization, you can also assign an admin to handle the user-management tasks for a specific sub org.
- **Applying Policy**: Sub orgs can be used to override the inheritance of privileges that come from the top-level organization. Sub organizations provide an effective means of applying the same policy to multiple users.
- **Organizing Users and Devices**: As organizations grow, it becomes important to group users and devices into smaller groups for manageability. You can divide the sub orgs based on geographic location, by department, or by product line.

Users and Organizational Units

You can add users to organizational units by selecting them individually or as a group and then moving the users to an existing organizational unit. In addition, you can create new organizational units on-the-fly when you move users. Users can belong to only one organizational unit. However, you can add users from different domains to your organizational unit. You can also give another user administrative rights to manage a particular organizational unit.

G Suite Global Directory

The *G Suite global directory* contains the list of your domain users. Everyone in the domain can view the G Suite directory by selecting the **Directory** link in the left navigation pane of their **Contacts** page. The G Suite global directory is integrated with Gmail™, Google Drive™, and Google Calendar™ so that your domain user's contact information is available for users to exchange email, share documents, and schedule appointments.

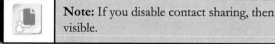
Note: If you disable contact sharing, then the **Directory** link on the **Contacts** page will not be visible.

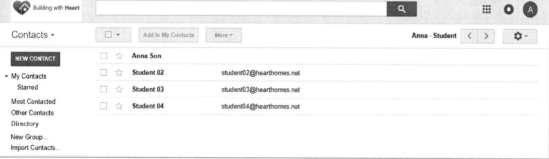

Figure 3-2: Domain Directory.

As the administrator, you can manage the Directory settings from the Admin Console by selecting the **Apps→G Suite→Directory** page. In the Sharing settings, you have the ability to enable contact sharing for your domain users and control the amount of contact information that is visible to users.

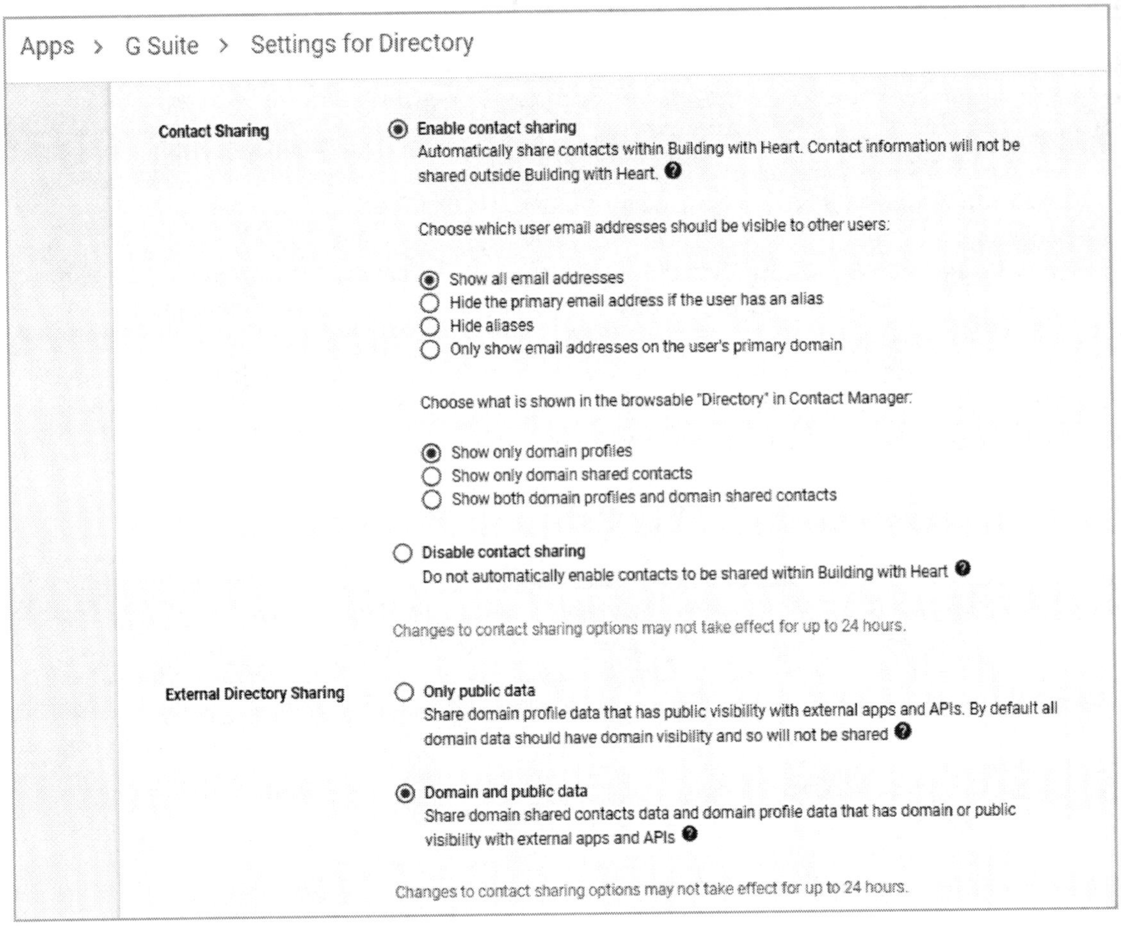

Figure 3-3: Enabling contact sharing.

Google Cloud Directory Sync

The *Google Cloud Directory Sync (GCDS)* tool enables you to keep your G Suite Directory in sync with a Microsoft® Active Directory®, an IBM® Domino®, or a *Lightweight Directory Access Protocol (LDAP)* directory server in your organization. GCDS performs a one-way synchronization by pulling additions, deletions, and modifications from your LDAP directory to your G Suite account. The LDAP server data is protected for accidental change because you cannot use GCDS to push changes to, or modify, the LDAP server.

The following table maps the Google Domain items that are synced in the LDAP directory server with GCDS.

G Suite Domain	LDAP Directory Server	Comments
Organizations	Organizational Units	Users in the G Suite domain can be categorized and synchronized manually or automatically.
Groups	Mailing Lists	Only public groups are synced. Private, user-created groups are not synced by GCDS.
Users	User	Users are organized by their email address.
Nicknames	User Aliases	Multiple aliases will be treated as multiple nicknames.
Passwords	Passwords	Imports passwords as an attribute.

G Suite Domain	LDAP Directory Server	Comments
Calendar Resources	Rooms	This includes meeting rooms and equipment.
Shared Contacts	Contacts	Personal contacts are not synced with GCDS.
User Profiles	Extended User Information	This includes phone numbers, addresses, and other information. If Google+™ is enabled, then GCDS synchronizes the user information with the Google+ profiles.

Access the Checklist tile on your CHOICE Course screen for reference information and job aids on How to Create an Organizational Unit.

ACTIVITY 3-1
Creating Organizational Units

Scenario
As the administrator, you want to divide the Building with Heart organization into organizational units that mirror how your people work. Currently, you have a group involved in the actual construction of the homes, another group focuses on spreading the word about your organization, and a third group organizes and manages the volunteer workforce.

1. Display the **Filters** pane in the **Users** page.
   a) Sign in as the Admin to the Admin console, if you are not signed in already.
   b) Select **Users** to open the **Users** page.
   c) Select the **Filters** icon to display the **Filters** pane, if it is not displayed.
   On the left side of the window, the **Filters** pane is used to change the users displayed.

2. Create a new organizational unit named **Construction**.
   a) Under **By Organization**, point to your organization and select the **Menu** icon.
   b) Select **Add sub organization**.
   The **Create new organization** dialog box opens.
   c) In the **Name of the organization** field, type *Construction*
   d) In the **Place this organization under** field, verify that your top-level domain *<your_domain.com>* is listed.
   e) Select **CREATE ORGANIZATION**.
   A message that the organization has been created appears at the top of the window.

f) Observe the new Construction organizational unit listed in the **Filters** pane.

3. Create two additional organizational units named **Marketing** and **Volunteers** under your top-level domain.

   a) At the top-level organization, select 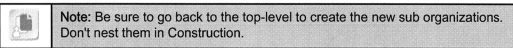 and then select **Add sub organization**.

   > **Note:** Be sure to go back to the top-level to create the new sub organizations. Don't nest them in Construction.

   b) Name the new sub organization *Marketing*
   c) In the **Place this organization under** field, verify that your top-level domain *<your_domain.com>* is listed.
   d) Select **CREATE ORGANIZATION**.
   e) Repeat the previous steps to create the *Volunteers* sub organization.

4. Move **Student 01** to the **Construction** organizational unit.

   a) In the **Filters** pane, select your top-level organization to display the users in your domain.
   b) For **Student 01**, select the **Menu** icon to observe the available menu commands.

None of the available actions apply to moving the user account to a different organization.

c) Point to the user name to toggle between the user image and a check box.

d) Select the check box to select the user.
   Additional user commands appear at the top of the Users page.

e) Select the **Move to another organization** button.

f) In the **Move to organization** menu, select **Construction**.

Note: While moving user accounts, you can create new organizational units on-the-fly by selecting **CREATE NEW**.

g) Select **CONFIRM** to confirm the move.
h) Refresh the Users page, if it doesn't happen automatically.
i) In the **Filters** pane, observe that Student 01 now appears in the Construction organizational unit.

5. Move **Student 03** from the top-level organization to the **Volunteers** organizational unit.

   a) Select the **Filters** icon.
   b) In the **By Organization** list, select *<your_domain.com>* and then select the icon for **Student 03**.

   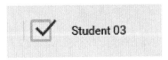

   c) Select and then select **Volunteers** and confirm the move.
   d) In the **Filters** pane, observe that Student 03 now appears in the Volunteers organizational unit.

6. Create a new user in the **Marketing** organizational unit.

   a) In the **Filters** pane, select the **Marketing** organizational unit.
   b) Select the icon. (You can only add one user at a time from within the organizational unit.)

c) Create a new user named *Student 04* and set a temporary password of your choice. Select **CREATE**.
d) In the **Create a new user** dialog boxes, follow the prompts to send an email to the new user.
e) Refresh the browser page to observe the users in each organizational unit.

TOPIC B

Manage G Suite Services with Organizational Units

G Suite provides the apps and services that users need to create documents, exchange email, manage their calendars and schedules, and sync their mobile devices.

Inheritance Hierarchy

You configure G Suite apps and services at the organization level and these settings are then inherited by users within that organization. When you create an organizational unit, it inherits the access settings from its parent organization. For example, everyone in the domain has access to Google Drive™, Gmail, and Google Hangouts™. If you create an organizational unit, any users you add or move to that organizational unit automatically inherit the settings for the three apps and services. As the administrator, you can change the access settings for a specific organizational unit and override the default Master setting that was inherited from the main domain.

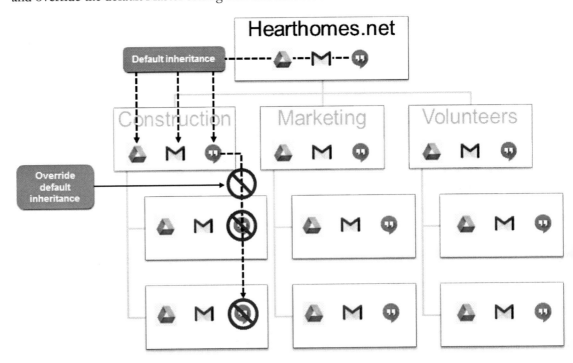

Figure 3-4: Inheritance hierarchy.

G Suite Apps and Organizational Unit Settings

One advantage to organizational units is the ability to manage access to the G Suite apps and services. From the Admin console, you can select **Apps→G Suite** to display the **G Suite** page. From this page, you can control the access to the apps and services at the organization or sub organization level. You can also use the **Add Services** button in the toolbar to add other paid services, such as Vault or G Suite Marketplace.

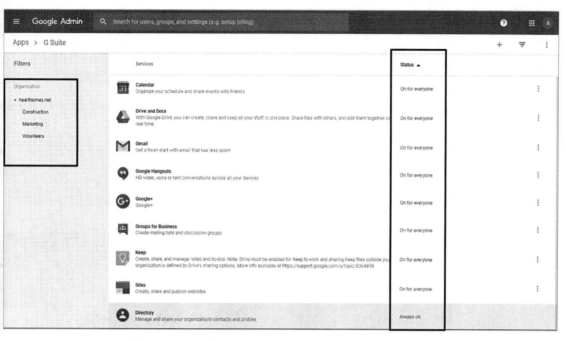

Figure 3-5: Turning off service settings.

Google Services

The nine core G Suite apps are Calendar, Drive and Docs, Gmail, Google Hangouts, Google+, Groups for Business, Keep, Sites, and Directory. The apps are configured and managed by a variety of Google services; 56 to be exact. Some of the additional Google services included on the **Additional Google services** page include:

- Blogger™
- Chrome Web Store
- Google AdSense™
- Google AdWords™
- Google Analytics™
- Google Chrome Sync
- Google Developers Console
- Google Groups™
- Google Wallet™
- Google Location History™
- Picasa Web Albums™
- YouTube™

 Note: To learn more about how to add third-party apps, check out the LearnTO **Evaluate Google Marketplace Apps** presentation from the **LearnTO** tile on the CHOICE Course screen.

Google Services Settings

By default, most of the Google services are turned on and available for users in your G Suite domain. As the administrator, you can control the service availability to users either individually from the user profile or collectively from the **Services** page. On the **Services** page, the Master setting applies to everyone in the organization and is inherited by the organizational units. If you plan to turn off services, it's important to do so before users are actively using the services, or you run the risk of users reacting negatively to having their access revoked.

You can configure Services by organizational unit. For some services, you can override the inherited access setting and enable the service for just a selected organizational unit. For example, you may want to turn off the Sites apps for users in the Construction organizational unit while it remains on for the rest of the organization.

You can change the scope of different Google services to:

- ON for everyone
- ON for some organizations
- OFF

If you set the setting to ON for some organizations, you can then choose which organizations should receive their own settings, and which should inherit from the parent organization.

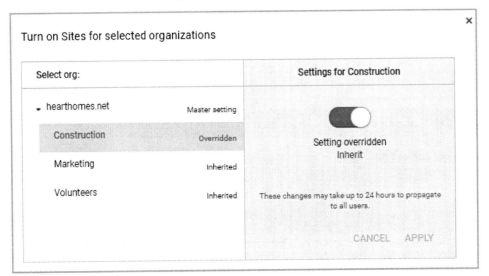

Figure 3-6: Turning off Sites for the Construction organizational unit.

 Access the Checklist tile on your CHOICE Course screen for reference information and job aids on **How to Manage Organizational Unit Settings.**

ACTIVITY 3-2
Using an Organizational Unit to Assign User Permissions

Scenario

There has been an increase in the amount of data and files leaking out of your organization without approval. This has become a concern to you and others in the senior management group. Knowing that the Volunteers group works closely with non-domain users, you can turn off Drive to help you get a handle on how the data might be leaking. Once the source of the leak is found, you can turn on Drive again.

1. View the default settings for the **Drive** service.
    a) From the Admin console dashboard, select **Apps**.
    b) Select **G Suite**.
       The G Suite Apps services are listed alphabetically and the **Status** column displays whether the service is OFF, ON for everyone, or ON for some organizations.
    c) Select **Drive and Docs** to open its page.
       The header portion of the Drive and Docs page contains the name of the service, its status, and a link to the domain sites. This page contains links to settings that you can use to configure rights and privileges.

2. Restrict the users in the **Volunteers** organization from accessing Drive by turning it off.
    a) In the upper-right corner of the **Drive and Docs** page, select the **Menu** icon.

    b) Select **ON for some organizations**.

c) Observe the **Master setting** for *<your_domain.com>*.

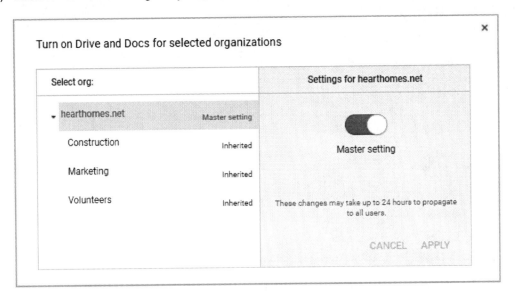

Drive and Docs is turned on (indicated by blue) for *<your_domain.com>* and all of the sub organizations inherit this setting.

d) Under **Select org**, select **Volunteers**.

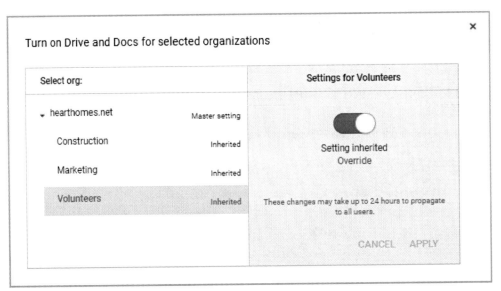

To change the settings for the selected Volunteers org, you need to override the inherited setting.

e) Under **Settings for Volunteers**, select **Override**.

The setting can now be changed.

f) Select the blue area of the slider to override the master setting and turn off Drive and Docs for Volunteers.

g) Select **APPLY**.

 Note: Changes might take up to 24 hours to propagate to users.

h) To confirm turning off Drive for Volunteers, select **TURN OFF**.
i) Close the open dialog box and observe the Drive and Docs status.

The **Status** column displays **On for selected orgs** now.

3. **Move Student 03 from Volunteers sub organization to the top-level organization.**

a) Select the **Navigation** menu icon and then select **Users**.
b) In the **Filters** pane, under **By Organization**, select **Volunteers** to display the users in that sub organization.
c) Select **Student 03** to open the profile page.

 Note: If you expand the "G Suite services enabled" section, you will see that Drive is still turned on because it takes 24 hours for the change to propagate.

d) Select [icon] and select the top-level domain (*<your_domain.com>*). Select **CONFIRM** to confirm moving the user.
Student 03 now has access to Drive and Docs again because it's no longer a member of the restricted Volunteers sub organization.
e) View the **Users** list to verify that Student 03 now belongs to the top-level organization. The Volunteers sub organization should be empty.
f) Select **SAVE**.

4. Return to the Admin console **Home** page, and close the web browser.

Summary

In this lesson, you learned about creating organizational units in your domain. You examined how to move users into the organizational units based on their shared needs for access to apps and services. Additionally, you controlled all of the users in a organizational unit by modifying the settings for one particular organizational unit.

Share with others how organizational units can be beneficial to your organization.

Have you used the Google Cloud Directory Sync (GCDS) to integrate your Active Directory or LDAP data into your G Suite domain? If so, what are the challenges of integration?

Note: Check your CHOICE Course screen for opportunities to interact with your classmates, peers, and the larger CHOICE online community about the topics covered in this course or other topics you are interested in. From the Course screen you can also access available resources for a more continuous learning experience.

4 Configuring Drive Storage and Sharing

Lesson Time: 1 hour, 15 minutes

Lesson Introduction

After creating sub organizations in your domain, you can use these groups to refine the management of users' Drive storage and sharing. Google Drive™ provides cloud-based storage for users in your domain that they can access while at their desk or on the move. As one of the services of the domain, you can also configure Drive to manage its use.

Lesson Objectives

In this lesson, you will:

- Configure Drive storage for multiple users.
- Configure Drive sharing.

TOPIC A

Configure Drive Storage Settings

You can access your Drive files and folders by using your web browser or opening the Google Drive folder on your computer. Either method will open Drive and Google™ keeps the files on the web and on your computer in sync.

Google Drive Interface

Google Drive is the central storage location for documents and files. With G Suite Basic, each user is allowed up to 30 GB of storage. In G Suite Business, users have unlimited storage if there are more than five users; fewer than five users, the storage is 1 TB per user. As the administrator, you can purchase additional storage and assign it to selected users, or you can enable users to purchase additional storage for themselves. In addition to accessing your Drive files through the web browser, you can also install Google Drive on a computer or a mobile device. Each user must have a Google account and sign-in credentials to use Google Drive.

When Drive is opened, you can identify its connection to your G Suite account by the customized company logo and the extended web URL. As a user, you can upload, create, save, edit, rename, and delete files by using the Drive app.

Figure 4-1: Drive app interface.

Drive App Settings

As the administrator using the Admin console dashboard controls, you can manage the Google Drive settings and policies for the domain. Some of the administrative tasks include:

- Monitoring individual and overall storage usage
- Enabling sharing policies
- Transferring ownership of files between users
- Configuring offline access to data

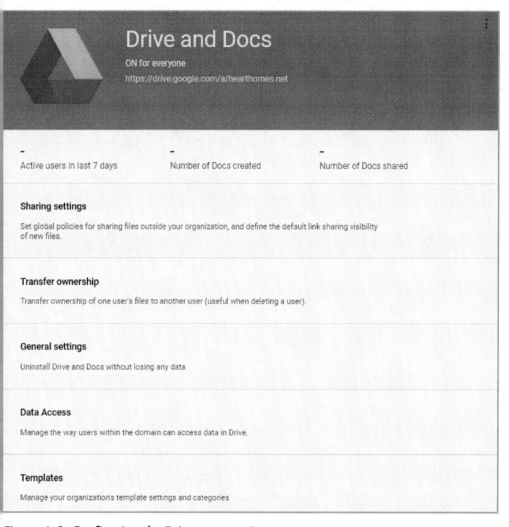

Figure 4-2: Configuring the Drive page settings.

ACTIVITY 4-1
Uploading a File to Drive

Data Files
C:\093008Data\Configuring Drive Storage and Sharing\Annual Report.docx
C:\093008Data\Configuring Drive Storage and Sharing\Donors.xlsx

Before You Begin
In the last activity of Lesson 3, the Drive app was turned off for the Volunteers sub organization; however, Student 03 was moved from the Volunteers sub organization to the top-level organization.

Scenario
You've been working locally on the files for the Annual Report that is sent to contributors and prospective donors. Because the annual report creation is a team effort, you know you need to share this document at some point to collect contributions from others. To prepare for sharing the file, you first need to move it to your Google Drive.

---

1. Open the **Drive** app settings and view the web address that identifies its location.
    a) Verify that you are signed in as the Admin and open the Admin console dashboard.
    b) Select **Apps→G Suite→Drive and Docs**.

    The Drive header contains the address of where Drive is located. Directly under the header is information about the number of Active users, number of docs created, and number of docs shared. Because your domain is fairly new, these document numbers will be low at this time.

2. As the Admin, open the **Drive** app and upload the **Annual Report** file.
    a) Select the **Google apps** icon and then select the **Drive** icon.
    b) Close the Welcome message, if it appears.

c) Select **New** and then select **File upload**.

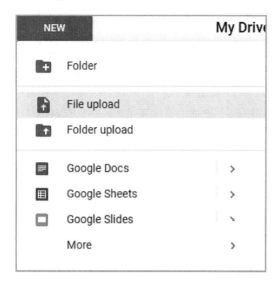

d) In the **Open** dialog box, navigate to the **C:\093008Data\Configuring Drive Storage and Sharing** folder, select **Annual Report**, and select **Open**.

e) Observe the **Upload complete** pop-up that displays the file name.

f) Point to the green check mark to see the icon changes to help you locate the recently uploaded file.

3. Preview the **Annual Report** document.

   a) On the Drive toolbar, select [≡] to view the Drive files in List view.
   b) Right-click the **Annual Report** document and select **Preview**.

   The document opens in a preview window with toolbar buttons that can be used to manage the file as well as manipulate the preview window.

   c) In the upper-left corner, select the **Close** button.

4. Upload the file **C:\093008Data\Configuring Drive Storage and Sharing \Donors.xlsx** to **Drive**.

Google Drive Installation

You can install Google Drive on a local computer from the Google Drive website at **https://www.google.com/drive/download**. Once installed, the Google Drive folder appears in File Manager just like other cloud-based storage applications, such as Dropbox. As an individual user, you have up to 15 GB of free storage for Drive files, email, and photos. With a G Suite account, you have up to 30 GB of free storage, and additional storage can be purchased at any time.

By using Google Drive on your computer, you have the same file management capabilities as those you have with Google Drive on the web. You can rename, edit, save, move, and delete files. Additionally, you can continue to access your files without an Internet connection.

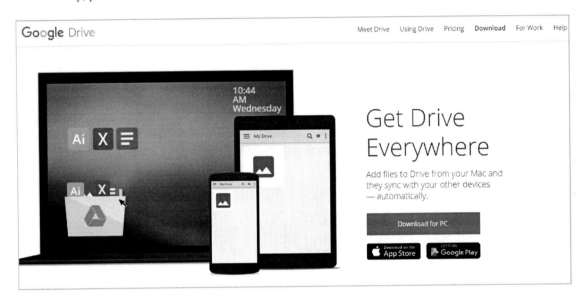

Figure 4-3: Google Drive web page.

Automatic Sync of Local Files

When you install the Google Drive client on your computer, the **Backup and Sync** icon appears in your system tray. By default, the entire contents of your local My Drive folder, Desktop, Documents, and Pictures are synchronized with your online Google Drive. (During setup, you will have the chance to change the default settings.) You can select the system tray icon to verify that the files have been synced.

A note of caution: During a mass deployment, after users have migrated to G Suite and the automatic sync starts, the high volume Internet traffic might be overwhelming and cause a slowdown.

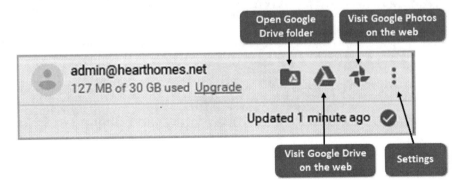

Figure 4-4: Syncing local Google Drive files.

ACTIVITY 4-2
Installing Google Drive and Syncing Files

Before You Begin

Google Drive is open on a separate browser tab.

Scenario

You want to be able to access your Drive files from your local computer. In order to do so, you'll download the desktop version of Google Drive for your PC.

1. From the browser tab, download and install Google Drive.

    a) On the Google Drive browser tab, select the **Settings** icon ⚙ and then select **Download Drive**.
    b) Select **Download for PC**.

    c) Select **Agree and download** to agree to the terms of service.
       Wait for the download to be complete.

2. Launch the **Google Drive Update Setup** to complete the Google Drive installation.

    a) Open the downloaded executable file **googledrivesync.exe**.
    b) When installation is complete, select **Close**.
    c) In the **Welcome to Google Drive** dialog box, select **Get Started**.

3. Sign in as the Admin and complete the Google Drive setup.

    a) When prompted to sign in to Google, follow the prompts to enter your admin credentials.

b) Read the message about choosing the local folders to backup and sync with Google Drive, then select **GOT IT**.
c) In the **Welcome to Google Drive (Step 2 of 3)** window, uncheck the Desktop, Documents, and Pictures folders, then select **Next**.
You only want to sync your personal My Drive to Google Drive, and not any of the files on the local computer.
d) Read the message about how to sync files, and then select **GOT IT**.
e) In the **Step 3 of 3** window, select **Sync My Drive to this computer** and select **Next**.
f) Select **START** and select **CONTINUE** to allow Google Drive to merge with My Drive.

The **Backup and Sync** icon appears in the Notification bar, and File Manager opens with the new Google Drive folder selected and opened.

g) In the Notification bar, observe the **Backup and Sync** icon. The arrows in the icon will rotate as the backup and sync is processing.

h) When backup and sync is done, select the **Backup and Sync Done** icon.

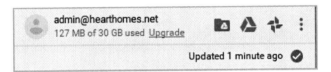

i) Observe the pop-up window.
The pop-up message displays any files that were updated, space usage information, and commands to work with Google Drive.

4. In the Chrome browser, close the **Google Drive** tab.

Storage Limits and Usage

Items that count toward your limit include Gmail messages and attachments, PDF files, images and videos stored in Drive, and photos larger than 2,048 × 2,048 pixels. Documents and files that you create with Google Docs, Sheets, and Slides do not count toward your storage limit. Additional storage can always be purchased. The Google Drive storage limits vary depending on your version of G Suite.

- G Suite Basic users each have 30 GB of free storage. You can purchase additional storage: 100 GB at $1.99/month or 1 TB at $9.99/month.
- G Suite Business users have unlimited free storage, if your domain has five or more users. If your domain has four or fewer users, then each user is limited to 1 TB of storage.
- G Suite Education™ users have 30 GB free storage.

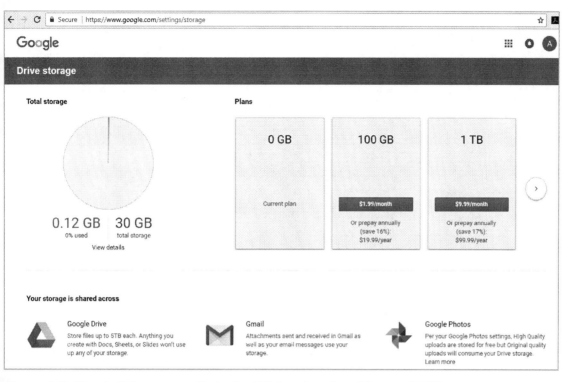

Figure 4-5: Google Drive storage limits for G Suite plans (as of August 2017).

The **User profile** page displays the amount of mail storage that is being used. You can open Reports from the Admin console dashboard to monitor the storage usage and which users are getting close to their storage limits.

 Access the Checklist tile on your CHOICE Course screen for reference information and job aids on How to View Storage Limits and Usage.

ACTIVITY 4-3
Viewing Storage Usage

Data Files
C:\093008Data\Configuring Drive Storage and Sharing\Marketing images

Before You Begin
You have downloaded, installed, and setup Google Drive on the local computer.

Scenario
You have been working on collecting image files that your Marketing group might use in future campaigns. Rather than send the large collection as an email attachment, you want to upload them to Drive and eventually share them. Also, as the admin, you are aware of the storage limits and want to make sure that users, including yourself, have not exceeded the allowable space.

1. Switch to the browser window and view the amount of available Drive storage space that you have used.
   a) Verify that the **My Drive** tab is selected.
   b) On the Drive tab, point to **Upgrade storage**.

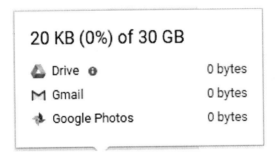

   A pop-up box appears with storage usage details.

2. As the Admin, view how much storage space domain users have used.
   a) From the Admin console, open the **Admin's User profile** page.

   The number of documents owned by the Admin is displayed under the user heading. The number of docs shown here might be different from your admin's number of docs.

b) Expand the **Account** section to view the **Storage** usage details.

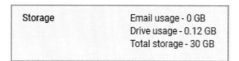

These storage numbers are unusually low because your domain is new.

3. Upload the entire contents of the **Marketing images** folder to your **Drive**.
    a) Switch to the **My Drive** browser tab.
    b) Select the **New** button and then select **Folder upload**.
    c) In the **Browse For Folder** dialog box, navigate to the **C:\093008Data\Configuring Drive Storage and Sharing\Marketing images** folder.

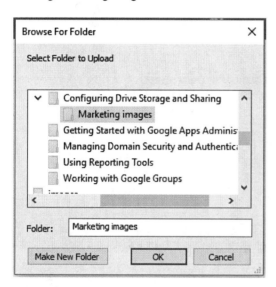

   d) Select **OK**.

You can see the upload progress of the **Marketing images** folder in the lower-right corner of the screen.

e) When uploading is complete, point to the lower-left corner of the screen to observe the amount of Drive storage used now.

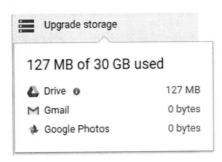

There has been a substantial increase in storage used.

4. **As the domain admin, view the Admin user profile to see the amount of storage being used.**
   a) From the Admin console, select **Users**.
   b) Open the Admin user profile and observe the number of **Docs owned**.
   The number of Docs owned has increased due to the addition of the **Marketing images** folder in Drive.
   c) Expand the **Account** section and scroll to view the Storage statistics.

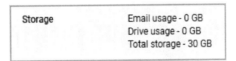

Because your domain and its users are new and have not uploaded a large volume of files, the Drive usage number is relatively low. However, over time, these statistics might indicate that the selected user is nearing their Drive storage limit.

5. **Examine the sample Highlights report shown here.**

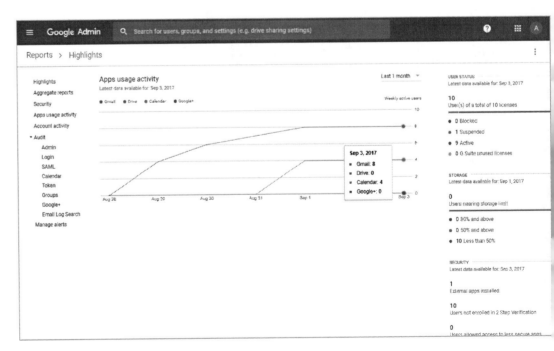

   a) Observe the **Apps usage activity** chart.

The Apps usage activity chart displays domain-wide statistics about how the users are using Gmail, Drive, Calendar, and Google+.

b) On the right side, observe the **Storage** data.
You can use this data to quickly see the users who are nearing their storage limit.

6. Close all browser tabs except the Admin console **Home** tab.

TOPIC B

Configure Drive Sharing

By default, everyone in your organization can share their files with other users inside of their own domain. As the administrator, you can modify the Drive sharing options to control whether or not files can be shared with people outside of your domain. Sharing files with non-domain users and having those files be visible to others on the Internet carries a slight amount of vulnerability or risk.

Google Drive Sharing Configuration

In G Suite, you configure the Drive sharing settings for the entire domain by using the **Sharing** options on the **Apps→G Suite→ Drive and Docs** page. By default, the ability to share files with users outside of your domain is enabled. The settings that you choose to enable in the **Sharing options** section will depend on how much you want to restrict or limit your domain users from sharing files with others, both internally and externally. In the G Suite context, *sharing* means inviting others to view, comment on, or edit a file that you own.

The **Access Checker** settings enable you to control the options available to users when they attempt to share files using another app like Gmail—instead of Docs or Drive. This feature checks the recipient's access level to the shared file. As the admin, you can determine which of the options are available to the domain user when they attempt to share a file.

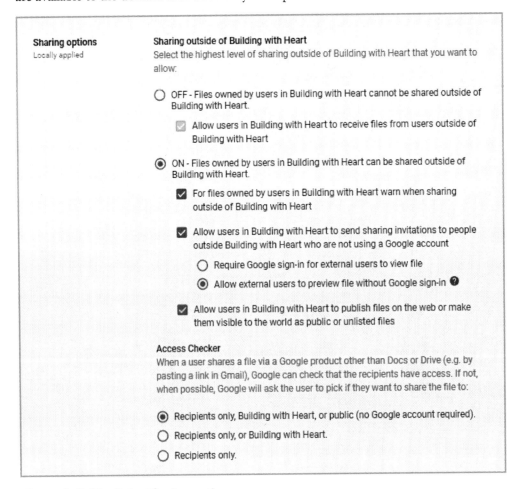

Figure 4-6: The Drive Sharing options.

The **Link Sharing** setting controls the visibility of the file. The link is the URL of the file that users can share with others, unless you've restricted them from doing so. The link sharing options are:
- OFF.
- ON for anyone in the organization with the link—must know the file URL. It's not searchable.
- ON for anyone in the organization—searchable and viewable.

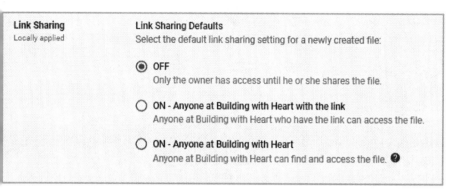

Figure 4-7: The Link Sharing options.

Note: If you have G Suite for Education, or G Suite for Nonprofits, you can also choose to whitelist (trust) specific domains and share only with whitelisted domains. The Sharing settings do not control users' ability to send files as email attachments. Even if you restrict sharing, users will still be able to send the files outside the domain to non-domain users.

When configuring the **Sharing options** settings, there are several decisions you must make that determine which settings to configure. The following examples illustrate a few situations.

Situation 1: Users in your domain are restricted from sharing their own files, but they can access external files that they've been invited to share.

Situation 2: External users can access a shared file, if and only if, they've been invited to share the file and they must sign in with a Google account. When sending the invitation, domain users will be warned about sharing files outside the domain.

Note: Keep in mind that a Google account can be created with any email address. It's not limited to only Gmail or G Suite email addresses. You can direct external users to sign up for a Google account without a Gmail address at **https://accounts.google.com/signupwithoutgmail**.

Situation 3: Domain users want to make their files visible to anyone on the Internet who knows the file name or has access to the link. To control what others can do in the files, they must set the view, edit, or comment permissions within the files.

Guidelines for Sharing Files and Folders

Note: All of the Guidelines for this lesson are available as checklists from the **Checklist** tile on the CHOICE Course screen.

The ability to share your files with others in your domain is an important part of using Google Drive and the productivity apps. However, there are some things to consider when making files available to users in your domain, as well as users outside of your domain.

Share Files and Folders

Use these guidelines when sharing files and folders:
- Use file sharing to collaborate and work on the same files with others. Up to 50 users can simultaneously edit or comment on a shared file. Beyond 50, users will have view access only.

- Assign the appropriate access to others for what they need. You can change the access at any time.
    - The most restrictive access, **Can View** access, enables others to only view the contents of files and folders.
    - **Can Comment** access enables others to annotate a file without changing its content. This access cannot be assigned to folders.
    - **Can Edit** access enables others to modify, share, and give others access to the file.
- Restrict access to only users within your domain when sharing sensitive or confidential company information.
- Control the access to the files by specifying that only the owner can change the access permissions.
- Use email or chat to send others a view-only link to a shared file.
- Share Microsoft® Office files by saving them to your Google Drive.
- Share multiple files by moving the files into a single folder and then sharing the folder.
- Turn off sharing for private files and folders.
- Use Google Groups™ to share files with a large number of people.
- Use group email addresses instead of individual email addresses to share files with many people.
- Consider using Google Forms if you are sharing a file to collect information, such as a survey or other polling-type data.

 Access the Checklist tile on your CHOICE Course screen for reference information and job aids on How to Configure Google Drive Sharing.

ACTIVITY 4-4
Configuring Drive Sharing

Data Files
C:\093008Data\Configuring Drive Storage and Sharing\Annual Report.docx
C:\093008Data\Configuring Drive Storage and Sharing\Donors.xlsx

Scenario
The Annual Report is almost ready to be sent to the contributors and partners of Building with Heart. There are some sections that still need to be edited before it's ready. The in-house volunteer coordinator will review and edit the volunteer section. And, the external accountant will finalize the financial portion of the annual report. To make the document accessible to everyone who is still working on it, you'll use Drive to collaborate on the report. Additionally, to track external users' activity in your domain, you will require that they sign in.

1. On the **G Suite→Drive** page, enable file sharing with users outside of your domain but require them to sign in with a Google account.
    a) From the Admin console, select **Apps→G Suite→Drive**.
    b) Select **Sharing settings** to expand the options.
    c) In the **Sharing options** settings, verify that **ON** is selected.
    d) Verify that the check box to warn users when sharing outside of *<your_domain.com>* is selected.

    > ⦿ ON - Files owned by users in Building with Heart can be shared outside of Building with Heart.
    >   ☑ For files owned by users in Building with Heart warn when sharing outside of Building with Heart

    e) Verify that the check box to allow users to send sharing invitations to people outside of *<your_domain.com>* is selected.
    f) Select **Require Google sign-in for external users to view file**.

    > ☑ Allow users in Building with Heart to send sharing invitations to people outside Building with Heart who are not using a Google account
    >   ⦿ Require Google sign-in for external users to view file
    >   ○ Allow external users to preview file without Google sign-in ❓

g) In the **Access Checker** section, select **Recipients only, or Building with Heart** to require recipients to have a Google account to view the shared file.

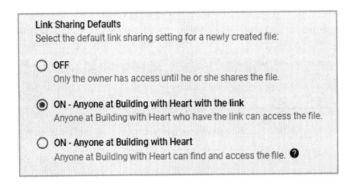

h) In the **Link Sharing** options, select **ON - Anyone at <your_domain.com> with the link** to enable domain users to access the file if they know the URL.

i) Select **SAVE**. Enter the Admin credentials, if prompted.
You need to allow up to 24 hours for the change to be effective.

2. **Use Google Drive to share the Annual Report file with someone outside of your G Suite domain.**

   a) Select the **My Drive** browser tab.

   If the **My Drive** browser tab is closed, select the **Google apps** icon and then **Drive** to open it.

   b) Right-click the **Annual Report** file and in the shortcut menu, select **Share**.
   c) In the **People** text box, type the email address of a person outside of your domain.

d) In the lower-right corner, select **Advanced** to display the **Sharing settings** dialog box.

In the **Share settings** dialog box, you can see the document link and the list of who has access. You can also invite more people, modify the access, and send a copy to yourself.

e) Select **Send**.
You receive a message to confirm that you want to share this file with someone outside of your domain.

f) Select **Yes**.
You're given one last look at the **Share settings** dialog box.

g) Select **Done**.

3. Share **C:\093008Data\Configuring Drive Storage and Sharing\Donors.xlsx** with an external user.

4. Close the **My Drive** browser tab.

Transfer of File Ownership

As the administrator, you can transfer the ownership of files from one user to another. When you transfer ownership, the original owner will continue to have edit access to their files. One reason for having two owners of files might be to provide backup in the event that one person is away or cannot access the files. Also, transferring ownership of files might be necessary when a person leaves the organization, but their files are company property that need to stay. As you prepare to remove a user from your domain, it's recommended that you transfer their files before deleting the user account so you don't lose the files.

 Access the Checklist tile on your CHOICE Course screen for reference information and job aids on How to Transfer File Ownership.

ACTIVITY 4-5
Transferring Ownership of Drive Files

Scenario

You are planning to take an extended vacation and will be away during an important board meeting. Knowing that the board members and other users will need to collaborate and work with the Annual Report and other documents during your absence, you want someone else to have access to the necessary files. You've decided to transfer the ownership of your files to the other Super Admin at Building with Heart.

1. From the Admin console dashboard, open the user profile for Student 02 to view the documents that they own.
   a) Select the **Admin console** tab, if it is not the active browser tab.
   b) Select **Users→Student 02** to open the profile.
   c) Observe the number of documents that Student 02 owns.

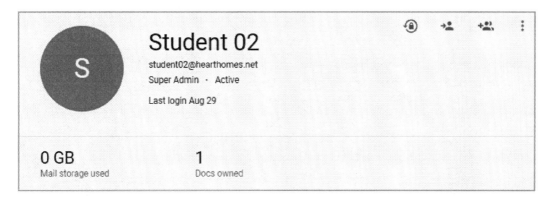

   d) View the number of documents owned by the Admin.

2. Transfer the ownership of the Admin's documents to Student 02.
   a) Return to the Admin console **Home** page.
   b) Select **Apps→G Suite→Drive and Docs**.
   c) Select **Transfer ownership** to expand the section.
   d) In the **From** field, type *admin*

e) In the **To** field, type *student02*

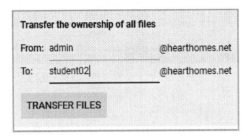

f) Select **TRANSFER FILES**.

According to the message, both file owners and you, the Admin, will be notified by email when the file ownership has completed.

g) Select **OK**.

3. **View the User profile for Student 02 to verify the ownership.**
   a) Return to the Admin console **Home** page.
   b) Select **Users→Student 02** and observe the Docs owned number.

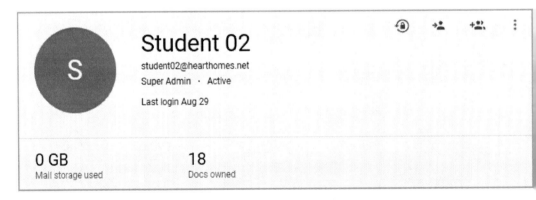

The Docs owned number has noticeably increased.

4. **Open the Admin's Inbox to view the Data Transfer message.**
   a) Select [icon] and then select [icon].

b) Open the message from **The G Suite Team** with the subject **Data transfer successful**.

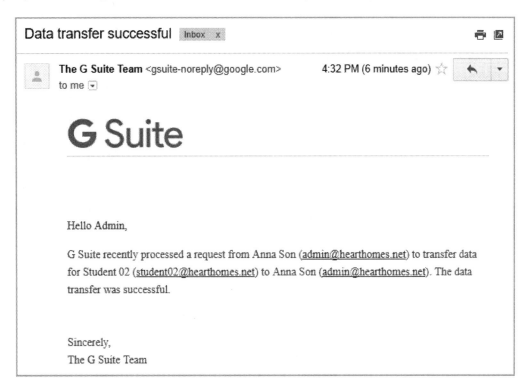

5. Sign in as Student 02 and view the Data transfer message and the new files in Drive.
   a) From the Admin's **Gmail** tab, select the **Account** menu and **Sign out**.
   b) Sign in as **Student 02** and observe the Data transfer message.
      The "Data transfer successful" message is similar to the one that was sent to the Admin who initiated the transfer.
   c) Open **Student 02's Drive** and observe the new folder.

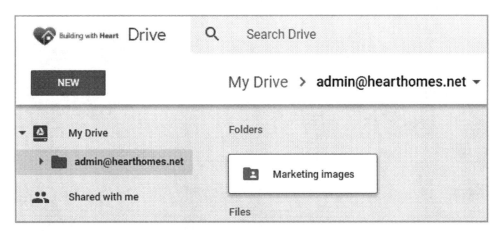

Because Student 02 was given ownership of the files, the folder appears in **My Drive** view, not Shared with me.

d) Double-click the **Marketing images** folder or expand the folders in the left pane to display the folder contents.

e) Select one of the files in the folder and observe the new Drive toolbar buttons.

These buttons indicate that Student 02 can edit the documents in this folder and the link is searchable by anyone in *<your_domain.com>*.

f) Close all Drive and Gmail browser tabs.

Summary

In this lesson, you learned about Google Drive storage and monitoring users' storage limits and usage. You also examined the benefit of using an organizational unit policy to manage your users' Drive limits. Finally, you configured Drive sharing for the users in your domain and transferred the ownership of files from one user to another.

Share your experiences of managing Google Drive for users.

Why would you transfer ownership of files between users?

Note: Check your CHOICE Course screen for opportunities to interact with your classmates, peers, and the larger CHOICE online community about the topics covered in this course or other topics you are interested in. From the Course screen you can also access available resources for a more continuous learning experience.

5 Managing Mail Routing, Delivery, and Filtering

Lesson Time: 3 hours

Lesson Introduction

Next to managing user accounts, maintaining the smooth delivery of mail is an important function for the Google™ account administrator. You need to maintain mail delivery and routing within your G Suite domain and between your domain and external, non-Google domains.

Lesson Objectives

In this lesson, you will:

- Set up and configure mail routing and delivery for the G Suite account.
- Block and allow email from specific IP addresses.
- Specify the criteria used to reject or deliver mail messages.
- Migrate user mail from Gmail to your G Suite domain.

TOPIC A

Configure Mail Routing and Delivery

The smooth delivery of email is vital to organizations today. Many people find it difficult to be productive without their email functioning properly. As the administrator, it's your responsibility to maintain and manage the email delivery.

G Suite Gmail

Google Mail, or Gmail™, is a web-based email service designed for sending and receiving email. G Suite Gmail is one of the apps in the suite, and has access to the integrated features that come with G Suite. Users who are familiar with the free version of Gmail should be able to easily transition to G Suite Gmail. The major difference will be that their email address includes the G Suite domain name (@domain name) rather than @gmail.com. Another difference is the increased storage capacity. Free Gmail accounts have 15 GB of storage compared to the 30 GB for a G Suite account.

You can use the Admin console dashboard to set up, manage, and monitor your domain user's email accounts.

 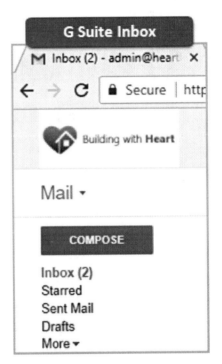

Figure 5-1: Comparison of personal Gmail and G Suite mail inboxes.

Inbox by Gmail

Inbox by Gmail™ is a tool designed to give you a new way to keep your Inbox organized. You can add it as a plug-in to your Chrome browser, or use the app on a mobile device. It is currently available through an early adopter program for G Suite users only. The administrator must enable it from the Admin console, then users can download and use it. The app synchronizes with Gmail, and the user can use either to access their Inbox.

The Inbox by Gmail interface has a simplified interface meant for mobile users. It bundles similar messages, provides at-a-glance highlights and search capabilities, lets you set reminders and snooze on specific emails.

G Suite Gmail Settings

By default, Gmail and its features are turned on, or available, for everyone in the organization to use. You can turn off or deactivate Gmail for everyone, and then activate it for only specific organizational units. You manage Gmail and its associated features from the Admin console by selecting **Apps**→**G Suite**→**Gmail** and selecting the **Menu** icon at the top of the page.

As the administrator, you control the configuration of your Gmail service and what users have access to and the actions they can perform in Gmail. However, you can give users some control over their Gmail environment by modifying the settings listed in the **User settings** section of the **Gmail** page. These settings include:

- Importing mail from non-Google accounts.
- Choosing a theme.
- Using read receipt requests.
- Delegating access to their mailboxes.
- Sending and receiving email using a Google+™ profile.
- Customizing the default name format.

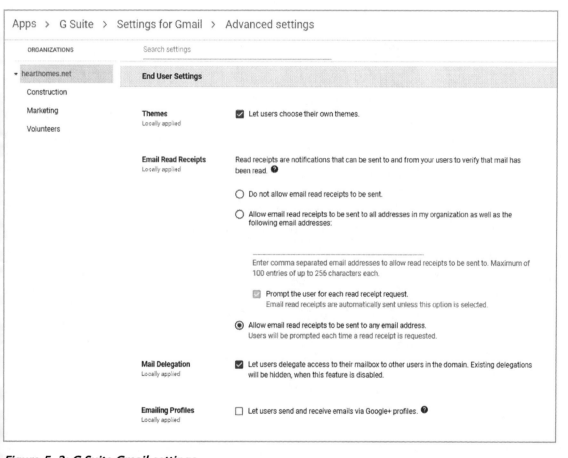

Figure 5-2: G Suite Gmail settings.

Gmail Settings

The following table describes the Gmail features available to G Suite domain users. All of the listed features are available in either G Suite Basic or G Suite Business.

Feature	Specs/Description
Email usage	• Email/IM storage limit for Unlimited edition is unlimited if domain has 5 or more users; if fewer than 5 users, it's 1 TB per user. Apps for Work users have 30 GB. • Attachment size limit is 25 MB (sending) and 50 MB (receiving). • Maximum recipients per message is 500. • Maximum recipients per day per user (outside of domain) is 3,000.
Addresses and mailing lists	• Email address includes domain name. For example: "*your_name@your_domain.com*" • Each user is allowed up to 30 email aliases. • Each domain can add up to 600 separate domains or 20 domain aliases. • Mailing lists are controlled by the admin as well as users.
Email and security and business controls	• Filters junk mail and blocks viruses. • Ability to turn off Google ads. • Apply custom filters and content policies. • Configure email retention policies. • Configure acceptable sources or whitelists. • Users can manage their own blacklists. • Compliance footers are enforced. • Google Vault is included in G Suite Business and available to purchase in G Suite Basic.
Access options	• Access from any web browser using computer or mobile devices (phones and tablets). • Access mail and Doc Editors when offline. • Voice and video chat available. • Can enable or disable IMAP and POP mail to use with G Suite apps. • Uses G Suite Sync for Microsoft Outlook® to manage G Suite mail and Outlook items.
Import and sync data	• Individually or as a group of multiple users from Microsoft Outlook. • Email messages from a web mail host. • Multiple users from IBM® Notes®. • Sync user data with LDAP server. • Use Exchange Calendar with G Suite apps.
Other email delivery options	• Catch-all address. • User and domain-level email routing. • Configure Inbound and Outbound gateways. • Configure outbound relay server. • Fetch mail from multiple POP addresses.

 Access the Checklist tile on your CHOICE Course screen for reference information and job aids on **How to Configure Gmail Settings**.

ACTIVITY 5-1
Configuring User Gmail Settings

Scenario

Because so many email messages are sent to outside volunteers and donors, your employees want to be able to track when their messages have been received and read. The people in your organization will be more efficient if you enable them to track their own messages by turning on read receipts. Additionally, to make it easy for them to use the Apps account mail as their primary email app, you can allow them to import mail from other web-based accounts so they have access to multiple mailboxes.

1. Verify that Gmail is activated for everyone in your domain.
    a) Verify that you are signed in as the Admin.
    b) From the Admin console, select **Apps→G Suite**.
    c) For the **Gmail** app, verify that the **Status** column displays **On for everyone**.

2. Configure the settings to use read receipt requests, delegate access to their mailboxes, and use Gmail offline.
    a) Select **Gmail** to open the **Gmail** page.
    b) Select **User settings**.
    c) Scroll to the **End User Settings** and in the **Email Read Receipts** section, select the option to **Allow email read receipts to be sent to any email address**.

    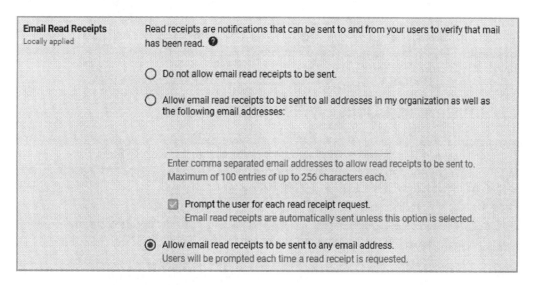

    Users will be prompted before a read receipt is requested.

d) In the **Mail Delegation** section, select **Let users delegate access to their mailbox to other users in the domain**.

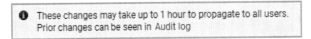

By enabling the **Mail Delegation** option, users can now give someone else access to their mailbox.

e) Scroll to the **End User Access** settings to verify that **Enable Offline Gmail for my users** is selected.

3. Save the Gmail settings.

    a) In the lower-left corner, observe the notification that these changes may take up to one hour to reach users.

    b) Select **SAVE**.
    A message stating that your settings have been saved appears at the top of the page.

Mail Fetcher

You can add up to five additional mail accounts to your Gmail account. The additional mail accounts can be Gmail accounts or from other email providers, such as Yahoo!® or Hotmail. When you walk through the steps to import the messages from the additional mail account, Gmail's *Mail Fetcher* service starts by importing old messages and then imports new messages as they are received.

You can stop importing mail from the additional account in Gmail. To do so, as a user open your Gmail **Settings→Accounts** tab, select the mail account and then select **Delete**. After turning off the mail import, you might continue to receive messages that were in transit. However, if you continue to receive messages several hours later, your other mail account might have started to automatically forward mail to your Gmail account. You'll need to modify the other mail account settings to make sure forwarding is turned off.

Mail Routing and Delivery Settings

The basic mail configuration is *direct delivery*, meaning that incoming mail is directly routed to your domain users' Gmail inboxes. If the email is addressed to someone who is not recognized in your Google account domain, the email will be discarded. This goes for names that are misspelled, as well as users who have been removed from your domain. In either case, the mail server does not recognize the name as valid.

For situations beyond the default direct delivery, you might need to modify the mail configuration settings. Possible advanced mail routing and delivery configurations might include the following.

- When a *catch-all address* is specified, any messages whose recipient is unrecognized as a domain user will be forwarded to this designated address. For example, if the name of the intended recipient is misspelled and therefore unrecognizable, the undeliverable mail is sent to the catch-all address. Some important considerations when using a catch-all address:
    - Use catch-all routing only if absolutely necessary.
    - Create a dedicated catchall address and clean it up on a regular basis.

- A catch-all email address can pose a challenge for spammers to try to guess and cause increased mail traffic.
- Increased mail traffic can negatively affect mail delivery or even cause an account to be locked out.
- When using a *mail gateway* server, mail sent to your Google domain will be filtered or archived before it's delivered. By default, Google provides the gateway servers for your domain's inbound and outbound mail. If you want to use your own gateway server, you need to configure it on the **Advanced Gmail Settings** page.
- You can configure different primary and secondary mail servers for mail delivery based on certain compliance settings. For example, messages containing questionable content or file attachments can be routed and delivered to a different server.
- When routing mail through non-Google mail servers, you need to create a list of mail hosts, or routes, on the **Gmail Hosts** tab. This list identifies the non-Google mail server or hosts that you have on-site or those you have used to exchange mail, such as a Microsoft® Exchange mail server. The next step is configuring the routing settings on the **General Settings** page.
- You want to implement email security best practices including using encrypted connections, alternate routes, and authentication.

Split Delivery and Dual Delivery Configurations

If you find yourself managing a migration from a legacy system to Gmail, you may want to take a more phased approach, in which you have some overlap with some users on your legacy system and others on the new G Suite system. Google supports such overlap through the following approaches.

- In a *split delivery* configuration, you can set up some users to receive their mail in Gmail while others continue to receive their mail through their legacy mail client. All mail passes through the Google servers, but email for users who have not yet been set up in the organization's G Suite account is forwarded on to the legacy server. This can be useful when you're phasing-in email migration on a group-by-group basis or when a portion of your organization must continue to use the legacy system to implement special handling for certain types of email.
- In a *dual delivery* configuration, mail passes through the Google servers and is also forwarded on to the legacy server. After you have imported legacy data for users into G Suite, they can switch from using the legacy system to using G Suite. After everyone has successfully transitioned, you can reconfigure email to deliver only to Gmail.

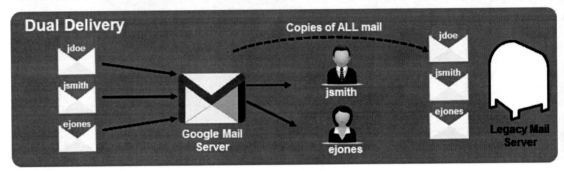

Figure 5-3: Comparing split delivery and dual delivery of legacy mail.

> Access the Checklist tile on your CHOICE Course screen for reference information and job aids on How to Configure Mail Routing and Delivery.

ACTIVITY 5-2
Handling Delivery to Unknown Recipients

Scenario

Normally, messages that are incorrectly addressed will bounce back to the sender. However, you'd like to see who is sending these messages and monitor the frequency. Designate one of the user accounts to be the catch-all inbox for unrecognized messages.

1. Create a new user account named **unknown address** to be the catch-all inbox.
    a) On the **Admin console→Users** page, select **Add user**.
    b) In the **Create a new user** dialog box, enter a first name of *Unknown* and a last name of *Address*.
    c) In the **Primary email address** field, enter *unknownaddress@<your_domain.com>*
    d) Select **Set password** and enter a password of your choice and confirm it.
    e) Select **CREATE**.
    f) Select **SEND EMAIL** to send the new user an email notification, if desired.

2. Use the Admin console to configure the **Unknown Address** account to be the catch-all inbox for unknown email recipients.
    a) Make sure that you are signed in to the Admin console.
    b) Select **Apps→G Suite→Gmail** to access the **Gmail** settings page.
    c) At the bottom of the page, select **Advanced settings**.
    d) Scroll to the **Routing** section and point to the **Routing setting** until the CONFIGURE button is displayed on the right side of the screen.
    e) Select **CONFIGURE**

3. Add a new setting to route unknown addresses to the catch-all address.
    a) In the **1. Messages to affect** section, select **Inbound**, and both **Internal—sending** and **Internal—receiving**.

    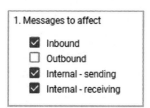

    b) In section 3, verify that **Modify message is selected.**

c) Under **Envelope recipient**, select **Change envelope recipient** and enter *unknownaddress* to the left of @existing-domain.

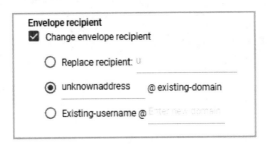

d) Select **Show options** to display options for account types to affect.
e) Select **Unrecognized/Catch-all** and uncheck **Users**.

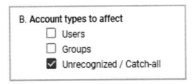

f) Select **SAVE** to add the settings.
g) In the lower-right corner of the screen, select **SAVE** to update the Gmail settings.

4. Test the new catch-all inbox by entering an unknown address in the **To** field of an email.
   a) As the Admin, open your **Gmail** inbox.
   b) Compose a new email message to *who@<your_domain.com>*. Be sure you do not address the email to the catch-all user.
   c) In the **Subject** field, enter *Testing unknown address*
   d) Select **Send**.

5. Verify that the email was delivered to the specified catch-all inbox, **unknown address@<your_domain.com>**.
   a) Sign in as the unknown address user.
   b) Open **Gmail**.
   c) Verify that the message sent to the unknown address appears.
   d) Open the **Testing unknown address** message and observe the **To** field.

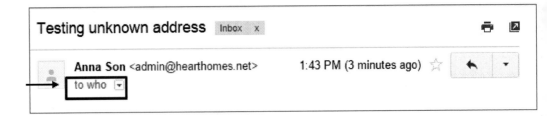

   e) Sign out of the Unknown Address Gmail account.

6. Sign in as the Admin and return to the Admin console **Home** page.

TOPIC B

Manage Blacklists and Whitelists

When you know that certain domains are only sending junk mail or spam, you can configure Gmail to block messages that originate in those domains. Conversely, you always allow email messages from trusted senders. These configuration settings can be your first line of defense when it comes to filtering out spam from users' inboxes.

Email Blacklist

Simply stated, an email *blacklist* contains the known IP addresses or email addresses that you want to block from exchanging mail with users in your domain. As the administrator, when you add specific addresses to the **Blocked senders** setting, you are blacklisting them. You can also block an entire domain and any organizational units that belong to that domain. To make exceptions to the blacklist, you can select the bypass option and create an approved senders list.

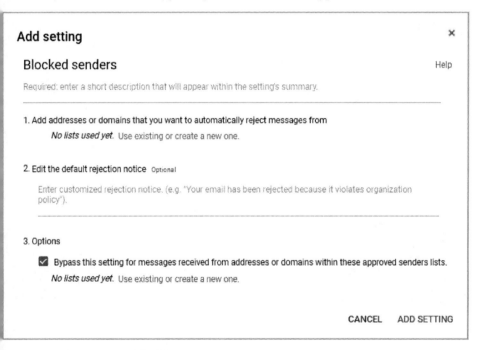

Figure 5-4: Creating a blacklist.

Email Whitelist

The email *whitelist* consists of the IP addresses that your domain trusts and accepts. Messages that are sent from this IP address will not be marked as spam. Keep in mind that whitelists are not exclusive; they are used to ensure that mail sent from them is allowed. If you have mail servers that are forwarding mail to Gmail, then they should be included in the **Inbound Gateway** field and not in the email whitelist.

MxToolbox (**mxtoolbox.com**) is a powerful lookup utility that can be used to discover a large amount of information about servers based on domain name, IP address, or host name. For example, when you know the domain name but not the IP address, you can use MxToolbox® to look up the IP address.

Spam Settings

In addition to creating a whitelist of IP addresses and a blacklist of individual email addresses or domain names, you can modify the general spam settings. By default, all incoming email messages are filtered by Google's spam filter. These spam filters are automatically bypassed for messages received by approved senders or internal senders. However, if you discover that too many spam emails are getting through the filter, then you can increase the filter's strength. You can also choose to move spam to an administrative quarantine.

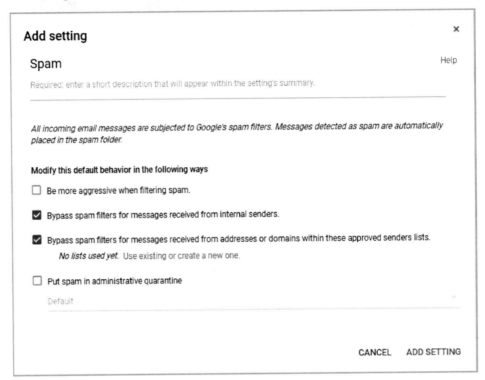

Figure 5-5: Adding a spam setting.

 Access the Checklist tile on your **CHOICE Course** screen for reference information and job aids on **How to Use Spam Filters.**

ACTIVITY 5-3
Creating an Email Blacklist

Scenario
Your organization wants to block known marketing firms from filling up your users' inboxes with junk mail. You've been reading about an online utility called MxToolbox that can be used to discover IP addresses.

1. Identify one classroom domain to represent a spam-producing domain and create a blacklist named **untrusted**.
   a) From the Admin console, select **Apps→G Suite→Gmail**.
   b) Select **Advanced settings**.
   c) On the **Advanced settings** page, scroll down to display the **Blocked senders** section.
   d) Point to the **Blocked senders** section until the **CONFIGURE** button appears.

   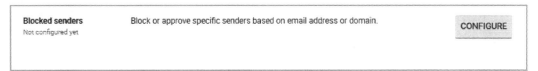

   e) Select the **CONFIGURE** button to open the **Add setting** dialog box.
   f) Under **Blocked senders**, enter *not trusted* as a short description.
   g) Select the **Use existing or create a new one.** link to create a new list.

   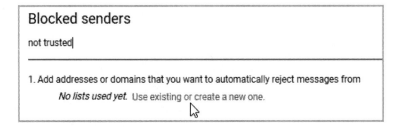

   h) In the **Create new list** field, enter *untrusted*

   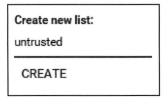

   i) Select **CREATE**. Sign in as the Admin if you are prompted to do so.
   The blacklist named "untrusted" now appears and when you point to it, additional commands, such as **Edit** and **Don't Use**, appear.

2. Add a user in a neighboring domain to your untrusted blacklist.

a) Point to the new **untrusted** blacklist and select **Edit**.

> 1. Add addresses or domains that you want
> untrusted (0)   Edit - Don't use

b) In the **untrusted** box, select **Add** and enter the email address of another student in class.
c) Select **SAVE**.
The email address now appears in the untrusted list.
d) In the **Edit the default rejection notice** box, type *Your email has been rejected due to organization policy.*

> 2. Edit the default rejection notice Optional
> Your email has been rejected due to organization policy.

e) Select **ADD SETTING**.
f) On the **Advanced settings** page, select **SAVE**.
g) Point to the new **Blocked senders** list.

You can make changes to the **Blocked senders** list by selecting the applicable buttons that appear when you point to the list.

3. **Test the blacklist by composing and sending a message from the blocked user account.**

   a) Ask the student who you've recently blocked to sign in to their Gmail and compose a new email message.
   b) Address the new message to *admin@<your_domain.com>*
   As a blocked sender, they will receive the following email message.

   c) Sign out from the blocked user account if you are using another user account in your domain.

TOPIC C

Filter Messages Based on Compliance Settings

Google provides compliance filters that enable you to filter and manage messages based on content, attachments, or objectionable language. For messages that match your filter requirements, you have the option to modify them or re-route them.

Content Compliance Setting

You can use the **Content compliance** setting to filter incoming or outgoing mail messages based on specific words or phrases. You can choose to filter inbound or outbound messages from external domains, or internal messages within your domain. You can add as many expressions as you want, and then specify whether all or just one of the criteria needs to be satisfied to filter the message. If the messages match your specified criteria, you have the following options:

- **Modify** the message by adding a header, appending the subject, changing the route, changing the envelope recipient, bypassing the spam filter, removing the attachments, adding more recipients to the delivery list, or requiring secure transport.
- **Reject** the message and return it to the sender.
- **Quarantine** the message and move it to the quarantine folder.

Naturally, you have the option to bypass the **Content compliance** setting for messages from a specific address or domain. After creating or modifying a **Content compliance** setting, allow up to an hour for the new changes to take affect.

Attachment Compliance Setting

You can configure an **Attachment compliance** setting to filter all messages that contain attachments of a specific file type, file name, or message size. You can create multiple expressions and then specify that messages must match either any or all of the expressions. The same options as in the **Content compliance** settings apply here. You can choose to modify, reject, or quarantine the filtered messages.

By default, all executable file attachments are automatically rejected.

Objectionable Content Setting

As the name implies, the **Objectionable content** setting enables you to create a list of objectionable words to use as a filter. You have the same options: modify, reject, or quarantine for dealing with the filtered messages. In the case of objectionable language, you might want to re-route the message to escalate the issue.

Access the Checklist tile on your CHOICE Course screen for reference information and job aids on How to Filter Messages with Compliance Settings.

ACTIVITY 5-4
Using Compliance Settings to Filter Messages

Scenario
The director of your organization has come to you with the problem of vital information being leaked to the public before it's ready to be released. While this isn't as devastating as selling company secrets, it can be embarrassing when the director has to answer questions that he's not prepared to answer. You can configure a Content compliance setting to filter outgoing messages that contain words related to an upcoming announcement and discover who has been sending the email.

1. On the Gmail **Advanced settings** page, add a new **Content compliance** filter.
   a) From the Admin console, select **Apps→G Suite→Gmail→Advanced settings**.
   b) Scroll down to the **Compliance** section and point to **Content compliance** to display the **CONFIGURE** button.

   c) Select **CONFIGURE** to display the **Add setting** dialog box.

2. Configure a new **Content compliance** setting to filter **Outbound** messages that contain either the word **giveaway** or **sweepstakes**.
   a) Under **Content compliance**, enter *Giveaway* as a description.
   b) For **Email messages to affect**, select the **Outbound** and **Internal-sending** check boxes.

   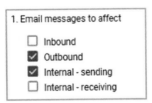

   c) Verify that **If ANY of the following match the message** is selected.

d) To the right of **No expressions added yet**, select **Add**.

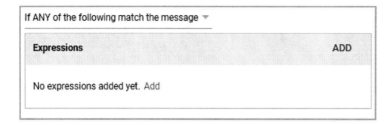

e) From the **Simple content match** drop-down list, select **Advanced content match**.

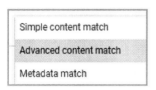

f) In the **Content** field, type *giveaway*

g) Select **SAVE** to create the first expression.
h) To the right of **Expressions**, select **ADD** and create a second advanced expression for the text *sweepstakes*
i) Select **SAVE** and observe the two expressions that you have created.

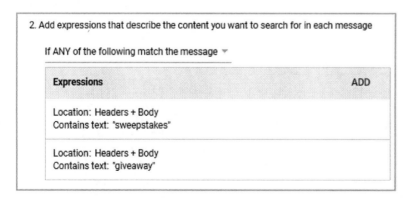

3. For messages that contain any of the expressions, quarantine them so you can see the senders and recipients.

a) In step 3, from the action menu, select **Quarantine message** and accept the **Default** quarantine.

b) Select **Add setting**.

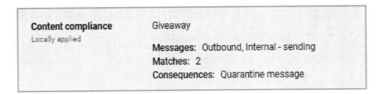

The new **Giveaway** filter appears.

4. Create an **Objectionable content** filter that quarantines messages containing the word **secret**.
   a) Point to the **Objectionable content** section and select **CONFIGURE**.
   b) In the **Add setting** dialog box, type *secret* in the required description field.

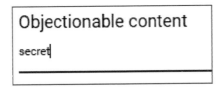

   c) For the **Email messages to affect** setting, check all options.

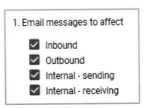

   d) Next to **Custom objectionable words**, select **Edit** and then select **Add**.
   e) Under **Enter words**, type *secret* and then select **SAVE**.
   f) From the list of available actions, select **Quarantine message**.

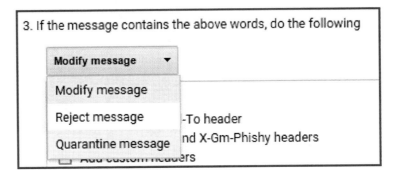

g) Select **Add setting**.

5. Verify that the two **Compliance** filters have been created and save them.
   a) Observe the two filters that you just created.

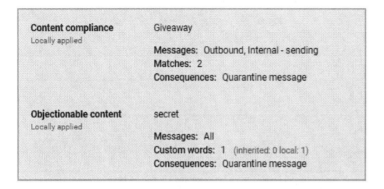

   b) In the lower-right corner of the **Advanced settings** page, select **SAVE**.

The Quarantine Manager

On the Gmail **Advanced settings** page, you can use the **Quarantines** tab to create quarantines. The Default quarantine is pre-configured to send the default reject message when delivery is denied. You can modify this Default quarantine, as well as create and modify custom ones. When messages violate your defined compliance policies and end up quarantined, you have two options:

- **Drop message** does not notify the sender.
- **Send the default reject message** informs the sender that their message has violated your compliance policy.

You can delete quarantines that you have created; however, if it is actively being used by a compliance setting, then you must remove it from the compliance setting before deleting the quarantine. The Default quarantine cannot be deleted.

As the administrator, you have access to use Quarantine Manager to handle quarantined messages. Go to **https://email-quarantine.google.com/adminreview** and sign in with your admin credentials. For each message, you have the option to allow delivery, deny delivery, or take no action so that the message expires after 30 days. When you release an inbound quarantined message, it is delivered to the intended recipient's mailbox. However, if you deny delivery, then the intended recipient receives nothing. For outbound quarantined messages, the sender's Sent folder contains the message; however, you must allow delivery before it can be sent.

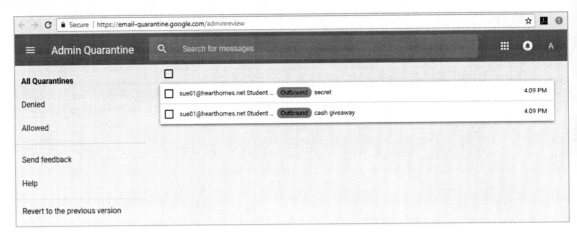

Figure 5-6: The Quarantine Manager.

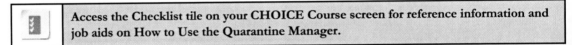

Access the Checklist tile on your CHOICE Course screen for reference information and job aids on How to Use the Quarantine Manager.

ACTIVITY 5-5
Using Quarantine Manager

Before You Begin
You have created two Compliance filters.

Scenario
Now that you've created a Content compliance filter for the words *giveaway* and *sweepstakes* and an Objectionable filter for the word *secret*, you want to test the filters.

1. As Student01@*<your_domain.com>* compose and send Gmail messages containing the Content and Objectionable filter words.

    a) Sign in as **Student01@***<your_domain.com>* and open **Gmail**.
    b) Send one message with *cash giveaway* in the body to a user in your domain.
    c) Send another message with *secret* in the Subject field to a user not in your domain.

2. As the Admin, verify that the Compliance filters worked and the messages were quarantined.

    a) Sign in as *admin@<your_domain.com>*
    b) Open a new browser tab and go to *https://email-quarantine.google.com/adminreview#* to open the Quarantine Manager.
    c) Observe the **All Quarantines** view.

    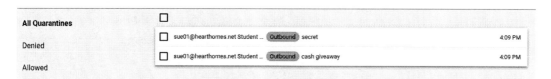

    You should see messages that are labeled as **Outbound** for the two messages that violated the Compliance filters.

3. As the Admin, use the Quarantine Manager to deny one of the messages.

    a) Select the quarantined message containing **secret**.

    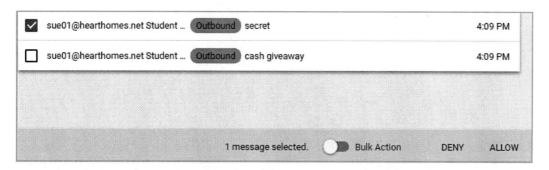

    When a message is selected, the **Allow** and **Deny** buttons become available at the bottom of the window. You can also use the **Bulk Action** button to affect multiple messages.

    b) Select **Deny**.

A "delivery failure" message will be generated and sent to the message sender, Student 01.

c) In the left pane, select **Denied**.

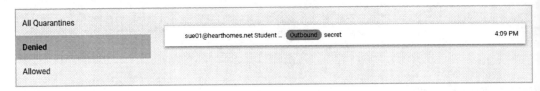

The quarantined and denied message now appears in the **Denied** folder. Likewise, any allowed messages would be moved to the **Allowed** folder.

4. **Switch to Student01@*<your_domain.com>* and verify that your message failed to be delivered.**

   a) If Student01's Gmail account is not open, sign in and open Gmail.
   b) View the "delivery failure" message.
   c) Sign out as Student 01.

TOPIC D

Migrate to G Suite Mail

As your G Suite domain grows and you hire more employees, you will need to help users set up their mailboxes. Many of them might want to transfer their existing mail messages into their new G Suite mail account.

Migration Tools

Another common G Suite Admin task is migrating users from a legacy mail system to G Suite. The process of creating new G Suite mail accounts and setting up users is fairly straightforward. The challenge lies in importing the mail, contacts, and calendars from the previous mail system into G Suite.

You can use the following migration tools to migrate user's mail, contacts, and calendar data to G Suite:

- Data Migration
- G Suite Migration for Microsoft® Exchange (GSMME)
- G Suite Migration for IBM® Notes® (GSMIN)

Migrate from Gmail to G Suite

The most straightforward migration is moving user account data from Gmail to G Suite. You can accomplish this basic migration by using the **Data Migration** tool from the Admin console. You need to create a G Suite account to provide a destination for the data. During the migration process, the user will need to sign in to their Gmail account and authorize access to their Gmail data. A progress indicator appears on the **Migration** page so you can monitor the migration progress.

Note: The **Data Migration** tool is used to migrate only email to a G Suite account. If you want to migrate users' calendars and contacts, you will need to install a migration tool, such as GSMME.

Access the Checklist tile on your CHOICE Course screen for reference information and job aids on How to Use Data Migration Service.

Migrate Multiple Users

You can use the G Suite Migration for Microsoft Exchange (GSMME) tool to migrate user's mail, contacts, and calendars from an IMAP server or a Gmail account to all versions of G Suite. GSMME supports a variety of IMAP servers, including Microsoft Exchange, Novell GroupWise, Cyrus, Courier, Dovecot, SunMail, and Zimbra.

Before you run the migration, you need to perform the following tasks.

- Download and install the GSMME tool at **https://tools.google.com/dlpage/exchangemigration**.
- From the email accounts that will be migrated, go to the account **Settings→Forwarding and POP/IMAP** tab and select the **Enable IMAP** radio button.
- Create a CSV file containing a list of users with their source email accounts, their passwords, and the destination email accounts, as shown.

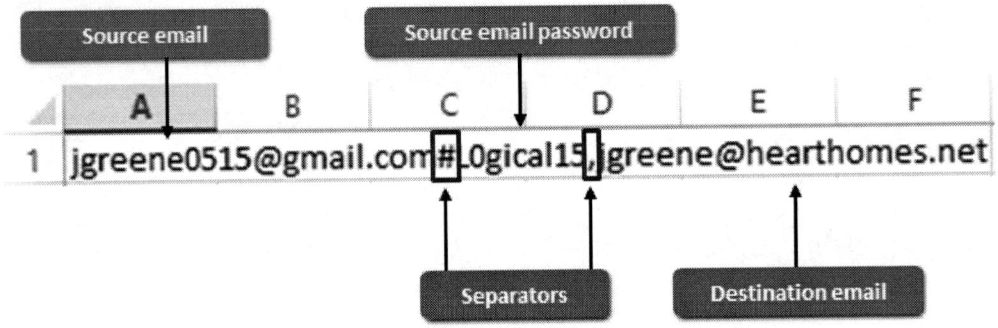

Figure 5-7: Syntax for CSV file.

> **Note:** Considering that this CSV file contains user accounts and passwords, it's critical that this file be kept secure and does not fall into the wrong hands.

After the preceding requirements have been met, you can run GSMME to migrate mail, contacts, and calendar items from the source domain to the G Suite domain. Depending on the server hosting your source email, the migration process can become complicated in a short amount of time. With that stated, the basic steps of the migration process are as follows:

1. Enable IMAP at the client.
2. Install the G Suite Migration Tool from **https://tools.google.com/dlpage/exchangemigration**.
3. Create a user list and save it as a CSV file.
4. Configure the Admin console to enable API access, enable your OAuth consumer key, and specify the API scopes.
5. Run GSMME tool.

> Access the Checklist tile on your CHOICE Course screen for reference information and job aids on **How to Use GSMME to Migrate Users Mail, Contacts, and Calendars**.

ACTIVITY 5-6
Using the Data Migration Service to Migrate Email

Before You Begin
Jane Greene's Gmail account was created during course setup and is ready to migrate into <your_domain.com>.

Scenario
You have hired Jane Greene as a new volunteer coordinator. She currently uses Gmail and would like to have her email migrated into her new email account at hearthomes.net. As the administrator, you can walk Jane through the necessary steps to give the Data Migration Service access to her Gmail account.

---

1. **INSTRUCTOR DEMO:** Enable IMAP access to Jane's Gmail account.
   a) Sign in as Jane Greene *<jgreeneMMDD@gmail.com>* and open her Gmail.
   b) Select ⚙ and then select **Settings** to open the **Settings** page.
   c) At the top of the page, select **Forwarding and POP/IMAP**.
   d) In the **IMAP Access** section, select **Enable IMAP** to give the Data Migration Service access to Jane's account.

   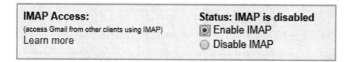

   e) Select **Save Changes**.
   You can return to the **Forwarding and POP/IMAP Settings** page to verify that the IMAP Status is enabled.

2. **CLASS:** As the Admin of your domain, send email to Jane Greene to populate her Gmail account.
   a) Sign in as the *Admin@<your_domain.com>*.
   b) Compose and send messages to Jane Greene's *<jgreeneMMDD@gmail.com>* Gmail account.

3. Create a new user account in your domain for Jane Greene.
   a) From the Admin console, select **Users**.

b) Select **Add user** and then type a First name of *Jane*, Last name of *Greene*, Email address *jgreene@<your_domain.com>*, and a password of your choice.

c) Select **CREATE** and then send an email notification to Jane.

4. Use the Admin console to configure the settings to migrate Jane Greene's Gmail messages to her new G Suite account.

   a) From the Admin console, select **Data Migration** to open the **Migration** page.

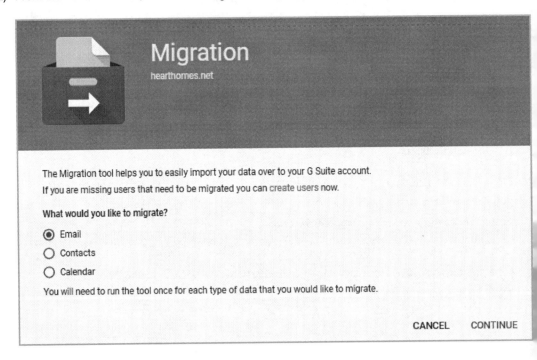

(If a previous migration screen appears, select ⋮ and then **Exit Migration** to start fresh.)

b) Under **What would you like to migrate?** verify that **Email** is selected and then select **CONTINUE**.

c) In the **Migration source** field, select **Gmail**.

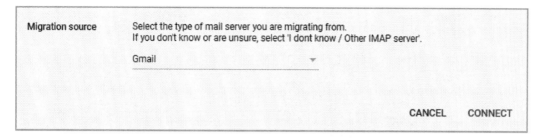

d) Select **CONNECT**.
e) Observe the default migration start date and options of what to migrate.

```
Connection successful! You are almost done.
You can now configure the migration setup.
In the next step you can select users* and migrate their email.

Migration start date    Select start date for migration. We will migrate your email from that date to the most recent,
                        starting with the most recent first.
                        Past 6 months

Migration options       Choose migration options as you need.
                        ☐ Migrate deleted email
                        ☐ Migrate junk email
                        ☐ Exclude following top level folders from migration (comma separated list)
                           e.g. Sent Items, MyFolder

                                                                                    CANCEL    SELECT USERS
```

f) Select **SELECT USERS**.
The Admin console tab is activated with the Data Migration Email page stating that there's no migration in progress.

5. Follow the prompts to select Jane's Gmail and obtain authorization to migrate Jane's mail.

   a) In the lower-right corner of the **Data Migration Email** page, point to and select the **Select user** icon.

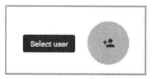

b) Observe the steps in the top half of the **Start Email Migration** wizard.

Start Email Migration

1. Enter Gmail address to migrate data from (source mailbox).
2. Authorize Data Migration Service to access the source mailbox.
    You must authorize Data Migration Service (DMS) to access the source mailbox for migration. You must log into that account to give this authorization.
    Please do the following:
        Click AUTHORIZE button and log in using the source mailbox email address.
        DMS will ask permission to 'View and manage your email'. Click 'Accept'.
        Copy the authorization code and enter it into 'Authorization Code' textbox below.
3. Select the mailbox to migrate to (destination).
4. Click on 'START' to start migration.

Note that authorization codes are valid for only 10 minutes from the time of generation and can not be used more than once.

c) In the **Migrate From** field, enter the email address and select **AUTHORIZE**.

d) When prompted, select the Gmail account to be migrated and then select **ALLOW**.

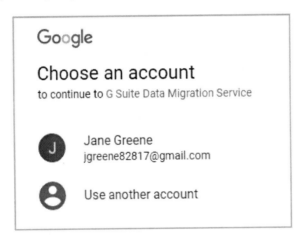

e) Select and copy the authorization code that is displayed.

f) Switch to the Admin console tab and paste the code in the **Migrate From** section.

g) In the **Migrate To** field, select the new Jane Greene account you just created.

h) Select **START**

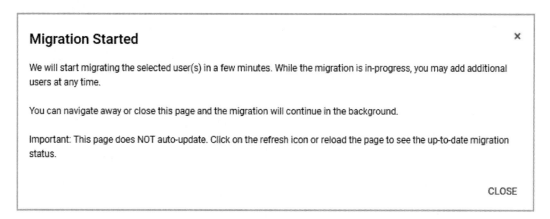

i) Select **CLOSE**

6. Verify that migration starts from Jane Greene's Gmail account to her *<your_domain.com>* account.
   a) On the **Data Migration** page, refresh the web page to verify that Jane's migration has started.

The migration progress is indicated at the top of the page and the **Status** column displays **Initializing** When complete, the **Status** will be automatically updated to **Complete**.
   b) Refresh the web page until the migration is complete.

7. When the migration is complete, send a migration report to the Super Admins.

   a) On the **Data Migration Email** toolbar, select ⋮ and then select **Migration Reports**.

   b) In the Migration Reports dialog box, under **Deliver to**, select **Super admins**.
   c) Select **SEND**.

8. Open your Admin Mail to download and view the Data Migration report.

   a) Switch to your Admin Mail and refresh the Inbox.
   b) Open the **DMS Consolidated Report** message.
   It contains a summary of the data migration along with an attachment that can be downloaded and saved to Drive.
   c) At the bottom of the email, point to the **MigrationReport<your_domain.com>** attachment.

   d) Select **Download** and then open the Data Migration report.
   The report is a spreadsheet that displays the user account details. Because you migrated only one user with very few messages, this report will be sparse.
   e) Close the report.

9. Verify that Jane's Gmail account data was migrated to her <your_domain.com> account.

   a) Sign in as *jgreene@<your_domain.com>* with the password.
   b) Accept the terms of agreement and change the password.
   c) Open **Gmail** and verify that her email messages were successfully migrated.
   d) Sign out from Jane's account.
   e) Close all open windows.

Summary

In this lesson, you learned about configuring and managing mail routing and delivery for your G Suite domain. You examined best practices for keeping your mail free from unwanted spam by creating blacklists and whitelists, as well as creating compliance settings that filter messages. Finally, you used the Data Migration Service to migrate a user's mail from Gmail to a G Suite account.

Share your experiences of migrating user mail accounts between different mail servers or services.

What types of mail filters or compliance settings do you use in your organization?

Note: Check your CHOICE Course screen for opportunities to interact with your classmates, peers, and the larger CHOICE online community about the topics covered in this course or other topics you are interested in. From the Course screen you can also access available resources for a more continuous learning experience.

6 | Working with Google Groups

Lesson Time: 2 hours, 45 minutes

Lesson Introduction

Google Groups™ makes it easy for your domain users to communicate with each other and share ideas by giving them a space to do so. In many ways, Google Groups is an online discussion group that can be as open as you choose. You can allow users the ability to create groups, or you can limit it to an admin privilege. Each organization must decide what's best for them and their users.

Lesson Objectives

In this lesson, you will:

- Create, modify, and delete groups.
- Use roles to manage permissions and group settings.
- Use groups to manage access to shared resources.
- Enable collaboration by creating a Groups for Business mailbox.

TOPIC A

Create and Modify Groups

Everyone is familiar with creating a group to make emailing more efficient. These distribution-list groups enable you to send a single email to multiple people. The second way to use groups has evolved from Internet communities that form around a common purpose. These types of groups want to be able to have online discussions, share files, and prioritize tasks.

Google Groups

A *Google Group* enables its group members to discuss topics and collaborate by posting and replying to discussion topics, participating in a question-and-answer forum, and managing task assignments in a shared inbox. When the Groups for Business service is enabled, Google Groups is available to all users in the G Suite domain.

All Admins can create a new Google group for their G Suite domains. There are two ways to create a group.

- From the Admin console, select **MORE CONTROLS→Groups** and then select the **Create Group** icon in the lower-right corner of the window.
- From the **Google apps** icon, select **Groups** and then select the **CREATE GROUP** button.

Either method can be used to create a group, but the interface for doing so and the configuration settings are slightly different. When Groups for Business is turned on, groups that were created from the Admin console are automatically displayed in the Groups directory.

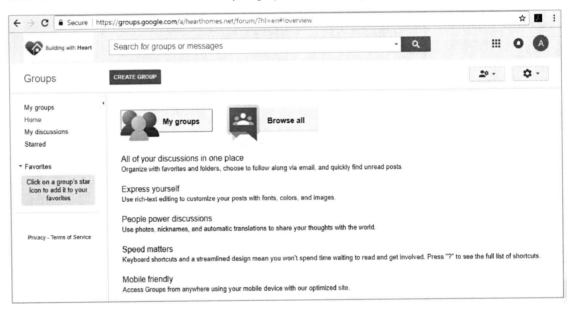

Figure 6-1: Google Groups.

Google Groups for Business

The Google Groups for Business service is on by default. When you create new Google groups, they appear on the Admin console **Groups** page, as well as in the **Groups for Business Service** page. The **View in Groups Service** link opens the Google Groups on a separate browser tab. In this interface, you have access to additional features for managing users, and creating and moderating groups.

Note: The difference between the Admin console Groups and the Google Groups for Business interfaces will become apparent as you work through the activities.

Google Groups Compared to Contact Groups

As a Gmail user, you are familiar with creating groups from your Gmail **Contacts** page. These groups function like a mail distribution list. You can add and remove contacts from the contact group without affecting the actual contacts in your Contacts list. Contact groups enable you to send one email to multiple people by simply entering the group name in the To address field.

In comparison, a Google Group functions as a discussion group for its members. There are different types of groups, but in the end, their goal is to facilitate communication and collaboration around a shared interest or project. Google Group members can be internal domain users or external users. The group membership is controlled by the group owner and the domain admin.

Admin Console Groups

You can use the Admin console Groups control to view the list of groups, as well as create and modify groups. Before you create a new Google Group, you should determine the purpose of the new group and what name to use. The following is a list of the group details that need to be considered before creating a new group:

- **Group name** should be descriptive and easily identifiable for its users.
- **Group email address** is automatically generated from the group name.
- **Description** defines the group's purpose.
- **Access level** specifies who can invite new members, view topics, post, or join the group.
  - **Public** enables anyone in the domain to participate.
  - **Team** enables Public-level participation, but only managers can invite new members.
  - **Announcement-only** enables anyone in the domain to join and read the archives, but only managers can post messages and view the members list.
  - **Restricted** limits the group participation to only members, and only managers can invite new members. Group messages do not appear in search results.

Figure 6-2: The Admin console Groups list.

The My Groups Page

To access your Google Groups, select the **Google apps** icon and then select **Groups**, or navigate to **https://groups.google.com**. This **Home** page is a portal to your groups, as well as giving you the ability to browse other public groups. In the left navigation pane, you can view your discussions, mark Favorites, and see Recently viewed groups. All of the groups that you belong to as a member, manager, or owner are listed on the **My groups** page. As the Admin, you have the ability to manage the group's welcome message and member list, and set permissions. However, users are only able to participate in the groups. To participate in a group, simply select the group name and begin creating or replying to topics.

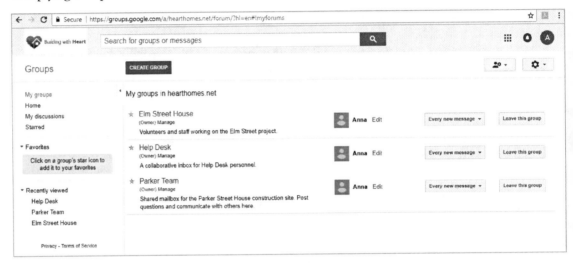

Figure 6-3: The My groups page.

Group Types

When you create a new group, you can specify the group type. The four available group types are email list, web forum, question and answer (Q&A) forum, and a collaborative inbox. With the group type selected, the applicable configuration settings are automatically made. The different group types do not necessarily build on each other in terms of functionality and privileges given to users and members. Rather, the different group types are used for different purposes.

Group Type	Description
Email list	Email is the only communication method, and users are not able to access the groups from the web address.
Web forum	Users can post discussion topics and reply to posts by using the web browser interface. Available features enable a moderator to facilitate the discussion.
Q&A forum	Users have the ability to ask and answer questions.
Collaborative Inbox	Users can assign tasks or action items, respond to topics as themselves or as the group, and indicate their completion status to work together.

> **Note:** To learn more about the different group types, check out the LearnTO **Use Different Google Groups** presentation from the **LearnTO** tile on the CHOICE Course screen.

ACTIVITY 6-1
Using the Admin Console to Create a Google Group

Scenario

After finding and "hiring" volunteers, the Building with Heart volunteer coordinator is responsible for supporting the teams of volunteers. It's important to clearly communicate details about the job such as the site location, the current day's activities, potential weather conditions, and transportation needs. The coordinator has asked you to create a web forum that the volunteers can use to share information about a particular job site. You currently have two home-construction projects underway, Elm Street and Parker Street.

1. From the Admin console, create a new group named **Elm Street House** with the email address of **elm-street-house@**<your_domain.com> and a useful description.

    a) If not already signed in, sign in as the Admin and open the Admin console.
    b) Select **MORE CONTROLS** and in the upper-right corner of the **Groups** control, select the plus sign to add it to the dashboard.

    You can also drag the Groups control to the dashboard.
    c) Select the **Groups** control to open the **Groups** page.

    d) In the lower-right corner, select **Create Group** to open the **Create new group** dialog box.
    e) In the **Name of the group** field, enter *Elm Street House*
    f) In the **Group email address** field, enter *elm-street-house*
       @<your_domain.com> is automatically added to the email address.
    g) In the **Description** field, enter *Volunteers and staff working on the Elm Street project.*

2. Specify the Access Level as **Public**.
   a) From the **Access Level** drop-down list, observe the available options.

   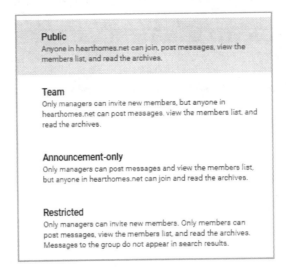

   b) Select **Public**.
      This will allow anyone in the domain to post messages, view the members list, and read the archives.
   c) Select **CREATE**.

   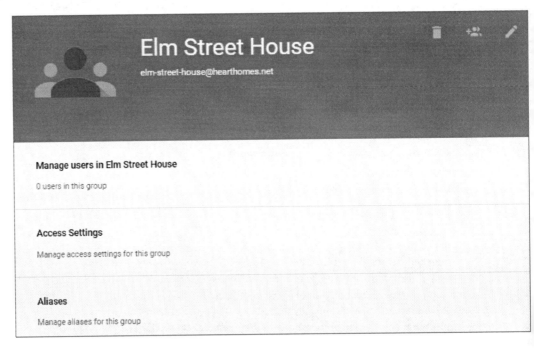

   The new group profile page for Elm Street House appears. You can use the links and buttons on this page to add and manage users, access group settings, delete the group, and edit the aliases and other information about the group.

Group Members

On the Google Groups Manage view, the Members list appears in a column layout that includes each member's display name, role, email address, and how they interact with the group. The buttons across the top of the page are used to manage members. You can use the links in the left pane to invite new members, directly add new members, view invitations that haven't been accepted yet, and view requests from users who want to join the group.

Figure 6-4: The Groups Members list displayed in Manage view.

ACTIVITY 6-2
Adding Group Members

Scenario
Now that you've created a group for the Elm Street building project, you need to add members. You already know of two internal people who are working on the project and should be added as members.

1. Add an internal staff member to the Elm Street House group.

    a) From the **Elm Street House** page, observe the icons at the top of the profile.

    You can use these buttons to delete the group, add domain users to the group, or change the group information.

    b) Select the  icon.
    c) In the **Add users to the selected groups** dialog box, type *student01@<your_domain.com>*

    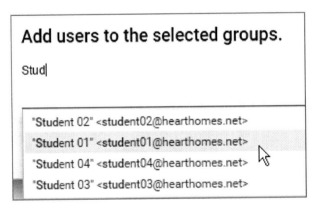

    As you begin typing the name, Google suggests users that match the characters as you type. You can select the name(s) from the Suggestion list.

    d) Verify that **Member** is selected.
    e) Select **ADD**.

    You are notified that one user has been added to the group.

2. From the Elm Street House profile page, access the group members.

    a) From the **Elm Street House** page, select **Manage users in Elm Street House**.
    A page with the **Advanced groups settings** opens.

b) Observe the **Advanced group settings** page.

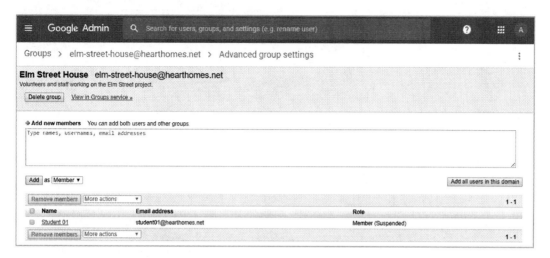

Student 01 is the only member of this group. From this page, you can add or remove members. The group name, email address, and description appear at the top of the page.

3. Add **Student 02** to the Elm Street House group.
   a) In the **Add new members** box, begin typing **Student02@**<your_domain.com> and select it from the Suggestion list.
   b) Verify that **Member** is selected.

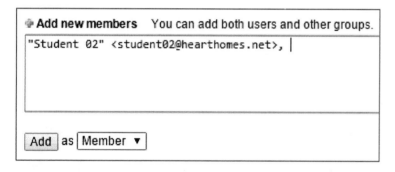

   c) Select **Add**.
   The Member list now contains Student 01 and Student 02.

4. Observe the **Add all users in this domain** button.
   If you select this button, everyone in your domain will be added in one easy step. When you do so, **All users within** <your_domain.com> appears in the Members list. If the group is intended to be used by your entire organization, then you could use this button to add everyone.

 Note: You can remove members just as easily by selecting the member's name and then selecting **Remove members**.

Google Group Settings

From the Admin console, the group settings and configuration options are somewhat limited. However, from the **Google Groups** page, you have access to an assortment of configuration settings. The following table describes the settings that are found on this page.

Setting Category	Used To
Members	View and manage the current group members, add new members by invitation or by directly adding them, and handle outstanding invitations and join requests.
Messages	View and manage messages that were sent to the group, but have been held up for further scrutiny.
Settings	Set email options, set moderation options for posts, and enable tags and categories.
Permissions	Set posting, moderation, and access permissions for the group.
Roles	Add members to one of the default roles (owner, manager, and member) for the group.
Information	Configure general settings that range from setting a maximum subject length to listing your group in the directory.

 Access the Checklist tile on your CHOICE Course screen for reference information and job aids on How to Work with Google Groups.

ACTIVITY 6-3
Adding a Welcome Message

Scenario
You want to provide users with some guidance and direction when it comes to using the new Google Group. The welcome message can serve this purpose.

1. From the **Advanced group settings** page, navigate to view the **Elm Street House** group in the Google Groups interface.
   a) At the top of the **Elm Street House** page, select the **View in Groups service** link.

   b) Observe the **Elm Street House group** page that opens in a new browser tab.

   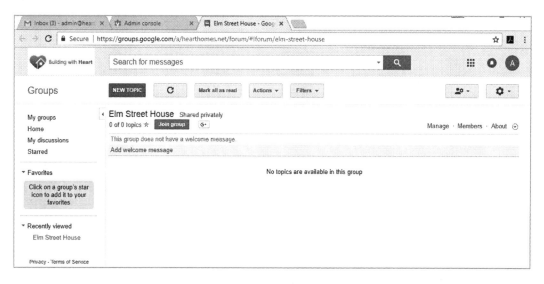

   As indicated by the URL in the **Address** field, this is the Google Groups interface that members see when they open the group page. As the admin, you have access to the **Manage** button.
   c) Observe the left-side navigation pane.
   This navigation pane contains links to My groups, Favorites, and Recently viewed. Because the group is new, discussion topics haven't been created yet. You can use the buttons across the top to create new topics and work with them. The new group page isn't very informative and there are no topics to read.

2. Add a welcome message to explain the group's purpose.
   a) Select the **Add welcome message** link.
   b) Type *Welcome to the Elm Street House Google group! Post your questions. Share job plans with other team members. Get weather updates.*

c) Select the first sentence and then select the **Bold** icon.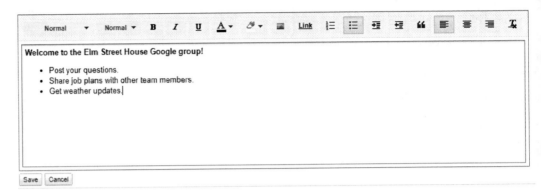

d) Place the remaining three sentences on separate lines and then format them as a bullet list.

e) Select **Save**.

 Note: After creating a welcome message, the option to edit or clear the welcome message is always available.

ACTIVITY 6-4
Modifying Membership

Scenario
When you created the new Elm Street House group, you were not automatically added as either a member or the owner of the group. As the domain Admin, you should definitely be a member. But, more importantly, you should be the Owner so you have the highest level of permissions and complete control to manage the group.

1. Join the group.
   a) Select the **Join group** button located under the group name.
   b) In the **Join the Elm Street House group** dialog box, observe your display name and your email delivery preference.

   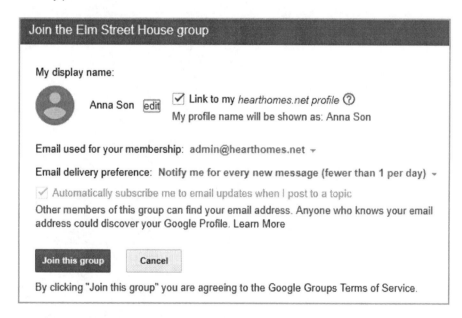

   You can change your display name by selecting **edit** and entering the name you want to use.
   c) Select **Join this group**.
   With the exception of the **Join this Group** button no longer visible, there's no noticeable change to the **Elm Street House** page.

2. Make your Admin account the **Owner** of the Elm Street House group.
   a) In the upper-right corner, select **Manage**.
   The **All Members** page opens and displays three members: you (the Admin), Student 01, and Student 02.
   b) Select your Admin account to open its details.

c) From the **Roles** drop-down menu, select **Owner**.

d) Select **Save**.
   The **All Members** page opens and your Admin account is now the Owner.

TOPIC B

Manage Group Security

While Groups provide an easy way to include many people inside and outside of your organization, they also give outsiders an opening into your domain. As the admin, it's up to you to control the access and permissions to the Google group.

Group Policies

Groups for Business is a service that can be enabled for users, configured, and uninstalled from your domain. As the admin, you can allow your Google Groups to be accessible on the Internet for anyone to view, search, and post. Or, you can limit your groups to only users in your domain. To configure the Groups for Business settings, from the Admin console dashboard, select **Apps→G Suite→Groups for Business**. Either the **Sharing settings** or the **Advanced settings** links will bring you to the configuration settings shown here.

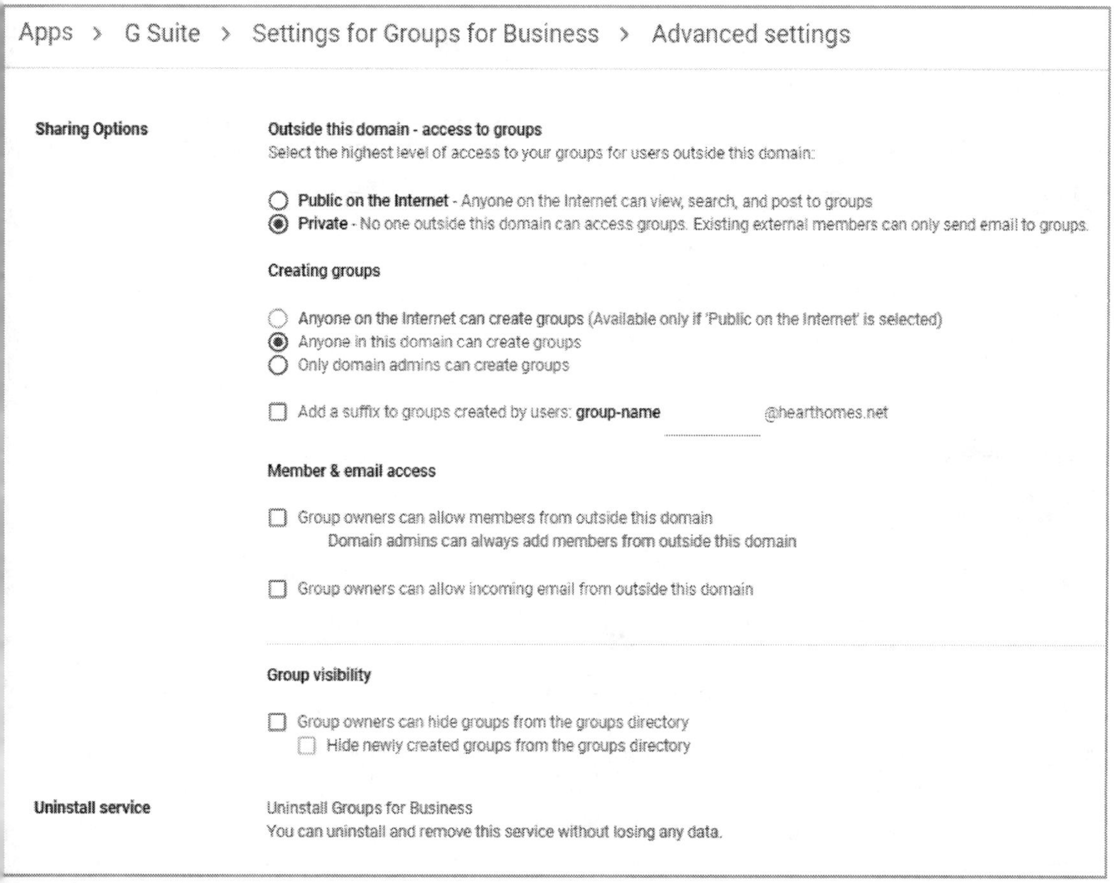

Figure 6-5: Groups for Business settings.

Group Limits

Google sets limits on the number of messages that can be exchanged within a Google Group. For example, there is a maximum number of message recipients per group, a maximum number of inbound messages per group, a maximum size of group messages, and so on. If you reach the limit, then group members might need to wait up to 24 hours before message activity can be resumed.

When you use the Google Groups web interface to invite members to join a group, then each user is limited to the number of groups they can join (30 per day) and groups they can create (5 per week). Additionally, there are limits on the number of external members that can be added (100/day) or invited to join (500/day) a group.

There are also limits on group membership. As the owner of the group, you count twice on the membership roll—once as the owner and once as a member. The maximum number of groups that each user can belong to is 2,000.

For more information and exact limits, refer to the G Suite Administrator Help documentation at **https://support.google.com**. When using a trial version, the maximum numbers are lower.

Group Permissions

Group permissions are divided into two main categories:

- *Group-wide permissions* are assigned to "Anyone" and apply to all members and visitors.
- *Role-specific permissions* are assigned to a role, such as "Member," "Owner," or "Manager."

There are two ways to access a Google Group's permission settings.

- From the **Admin console→Groups**, select the group you want to affect and then select **Access Settings**.
- From the **Google Groups Topic** screen, display the group to be affected and select **Manage** and expand **Permissions** in the left pane.

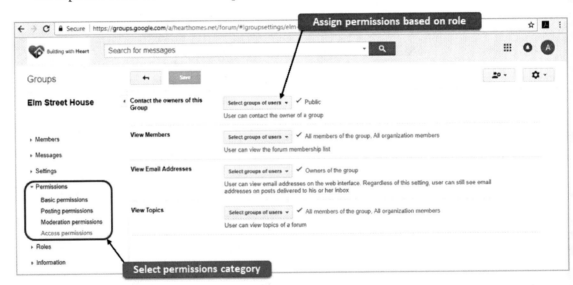

Figure 6-6: Google Groups Access Permission settings.

The **Permissions** settings are divided into Basic, Posting, Moderation, and Access. As the admin, the settings that you need to configure will depend on the actions that you are trying to control.

- **Basic permissions** are the default permissions that are configured when you create a new group. These permissions control who can view topics, post, join the group, and whether external users are allowed. You can even create a question for new members to answer, and base their membership on their answer.
- **Posting permissions** are related to how members interact with group topics, such as attaching files, using Me Too, posting announcements, and using canned responses.
- **Moderation permissions** are specific actions that a group moderator might perform, such as approving messages, deleting posts and topics, locking topics, and banning users.
- **Access permissions** control who can view the membership list, view the members' email addresses, view topics, and contact the group owner.

Note: You can see an exhaustive list of the available permissions in the Groups Help.

Roles

By default, the Owner, Manager, and Member roles are automatically created for a Google group. Only the group Owner has the ability to modify group Roles. You can edit the Members assigned to these built-in roles, but you cannot delete any of these three roles. Google provides a set of permissions that you can use to create a custom role for groups in your organization.

Permissions Assigned to Default Roles

The following table lists the permissions that are assigned to the three built-in roles.

Role	Permissions
Owner	• Add Members • Approve Members • Approve Messages • Attach Files • Ban Users • Delete Any Post • Delete Topics • Invite Members • Lock Topics • Modify Members • Modify Roles • Post Announcements • Sticky Topics • View Member Email Addresses • View Members • View Topics
Manager	• Add Members • Approve Messages • Attach Files • Delete Any Post • Delete Topics • Invite Members • Lock Topics • Modify Members • Post Announcements • Sticky Topics • View Members • View Topics

Role	Permissions
Member	- Attach Files - Invite Members - View Members - View Topics

 Access the Checklist tile on your CHOICE Course screen for reference information and job aids on **How to Manage Group Security.**

ACTIVITY 6-5
Managing Group Access Settings

Scenario
The Elm Street House group will be used by internal Building with Heart staff and external volunteers. When the group was created, only users in your G Suite domain could be added to the group. You need to change the basic permissions for the group to add members who do not belong to your domain. In addition, you want anyone to be able to request membership to the group. To determine if a requester really belongs in the group, they must correctly identify the Elm Street House building supervisor.

1. Modify the Groups for Business App settings and make the Elm Street House public to anyone on the Internet.
   a) Navigate to the Admin console.
   b) Select **Apps→G Suite→Groups for Business** to display the Groups for Business profile page.
   c) Select **Advanced settings**.
   d) In the **Sharing options** section, select **Public on the Internet**.
   e) Observe the **Member & email access** options.
   While you, as the admin, can always add external members, you might also want to give group owners the ability to add external members to their groups.
   f) Select **SAVE**.

2. On the **Elm Street House** page, modify the **Basic permissions** to allow external members.
   a) Go to the Admin console **Home** page.
   b) Select **Groups** and select the **Elm Street House** group.
   c) Select **Access Settings** to open the group in **Manage view**.
   d) In the left pane, expand **Permissions**, if it's not already expanded.

e) Select **Basic permissions**.

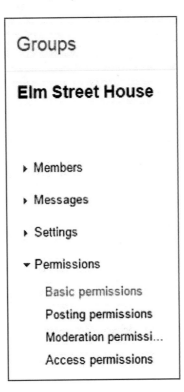

f) Select the **Allow new users not in** *<your_domain.com>* check box.

3. **Modify the setting so that anyone inside or external to your organization can ask to join the Elm Street House group.**

   a) In the **Join the group** section, from the **Select who can join** drop-down menu, select **Anyone can ask**. The "Anyone in the organization can ask" option is automatically selected too.

b) In the **New member question** field, enter *Who is the building supervisor?*

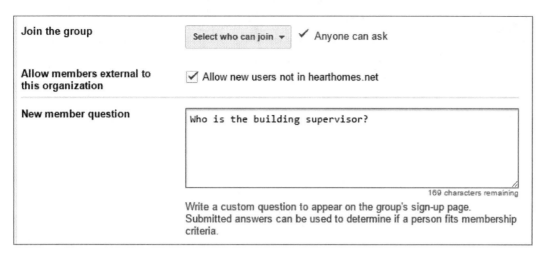

c) Select **Save**.
d) Refresh the browser page.

ACTIVITY 6-6
Inviting an External Member to the Group

Before You Begin
You have created a non-domain Yahoo.com account for Lydia Kim *lydiakimMMDD@yahoo.com* during course setup.

Scenario
Additionally, Lydia Kim has joined the volunteer team that will be working on the Elm Street House project. To make sure she receives communication about the project information, as well as helping her feel a part of the home-building community, you need to add her to the new Google group.

1. Invite Lydia, the external volunteer, to join the Elm Street House group.
    a) Verify that the **Elm Street House** page is in Manage view.
    b) Navigate to the Elm Street House **All members** page.

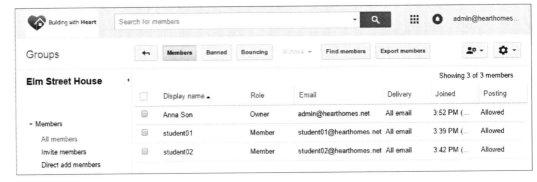

   The All members list is displayed and you are now listed as the Owner of the group. You can use the buttons across the top of the page to affect the selected members. Using the management links on the left, you can add new members by invitation or by directly adding them.
    c) In the left pane, select **Invite members**.
    d) In the **Email** field, enter Lydia's yahoo.com address: *lydiakimMMDD@yahoo.com*

e) In the required **Message** field, enter *Please join us!*

f) Select **Send Invites**.
g) In the **Verification** dialog box, check **I am not a robot** and follow the instructions to prove it. Select **Continue**.
h) When the "Invitation sent" message is displayed, select **Done**.

 Note: If you wanted to invite more than one person, you could do so now.

2. View the pending status of the invitation that was sent to the person outside of your G Suite domain.
    a) Select **Manage** to return to your Admin view of the Google Group.
    b) In the left pane, select **Outstanding invites** to see the pending invitation.

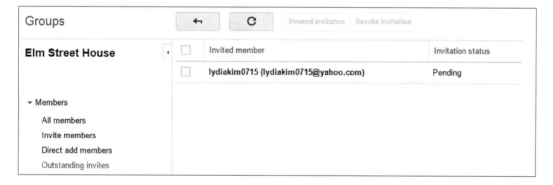

You can select the invited member and either resend or revoke the invitation.

3. (Optional) Switch to the external Yahoo! account to accept the invitation and join the Elm Street House group.
    a) In a new browser tab, go to **Yahoo! Mail**.
    b) Select **Sign in** and follow the prompts to sign in as **Lydia Kim** <lydiakim*MMDD*@yahoo.com>.

c) Open the invitation to the Elm Street House group.

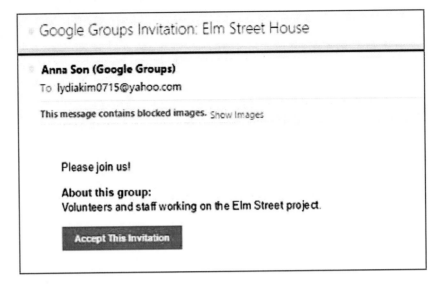

d) Select **Accept This Invitation** and observe the message that you have successfully joined the Elm Street House group.

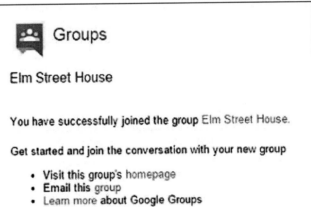

A new tab opens with a Groups message stating that you have successfully joined the Elm Street House group.

e) Close the Yahoo! Mail tab and the Google Groups tab.

4. **Switch to your Admin account and verify that the external user appears as a member of the Elm Street House group.**
   a) From the **Account name** menu, select **Add account**.
   b) Select your Admin account and enter the password.
   c) Navigate to the **Elm Street House** group and display the **Manage** view.

d) Display the **All members** list and verify that the external user is now listed.

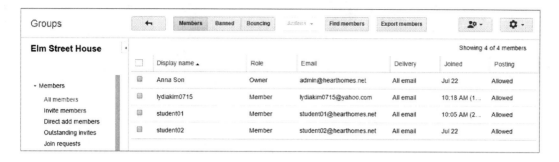

ACTIVITY 6-7
Requesting to Join a Group (Optional)

Before You Begin
Your domain's groups have been configured to be Public on the Internet.

You have a non-domain Gmail account for Jane Greene, *jgreeneMMDD@gmail.com*.

Scenario
You want to see how users are prompted for the new membership question when they ask to join a group.

---

1. Write down the URL for your domain.
   a) Write the URL in the following space:

   _____

   b) For classroom purposes, the URL is **https://groups.google.com/a/**<your_domain.com>.

2. Sign in as an external user and navigate to the group URL and locate the Elm Street House group.
   a) From the **Account name** menu, sign in as **Jane Greene** (*jgreeneMMDD@gmail.com*) using the exact email address and password from your instructor.
   b) In the web browser **Address** field, enter *https://groups.google.com/a/hearthomes.net* replacing the domain name with your domain name.
   c) In the **Search** field, enter *elm-street-house@hearthomes.net*

   > **Elm Street House**
   > You must be a member of this group to view and participate in it.
   > Apply for membership or contact the owner.
   >
   > Report this group
   > You are signed in as **jgreene0515@gmail.com**.
   > You can also try viewing this page as admin@hearthomes.net.

   When the Elm Street House group is selected, a page tells you that you must be a member in order to view and participate in this group.

3. Apply for membership in the group.
   a) Select **Apply for membership**.
   b) Observe your display name and email preferences.

c) Under the new member question **Who is the building supervisor?** type *Brian Wilson*

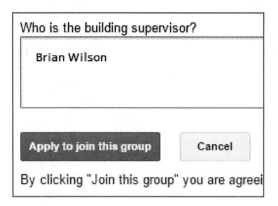

d) Select the **Apply to join this group** button.

4. Switch to the Admin account and approve the **Join Request**.
   a) Use the **Account name** menu to sign in as the **Admin**.
   b) Navigate to the **Elm Street House** group **Manage** view, and select **Join requests** to view the pending request.

   c) Observe the **Reason** column.
   It contains **Brian Wilson** because that was your answer to the new member question. This can be useful when deciding whether or not to approve a join request.
   d) Select the check box next to the requester's name.

   e) Select the **Approve applicant** button.
   f) Verify that Jane Greene has been added to the **All members** list.
   g) Close the **Group** tab.

TOPIC C

Share Content Using Groups

Google groups make it easier to manage the permissions and access to content for multiple people. This is further simplified when everyone in the group has the same access level.

Share Content with a Group

When you share content with a group, all group members will have access to the shared content. By changing the group membership, you can change who has access to the content. If the group contains another group, that nested group is given the same permissions as the main, or parent group. Using a Google group can be a more efficient way to manage access to shared files.

Some additional considerations to keep in mind:

- Content that can be shared in this manner includes documents, sites, videos, and calendars.
- As the admin, you can prevent group members who are outside of your Apps domain from seeing shared content.
- Members can include groups in addition to individual users. Those sub-groups inherit the parent group's access level.

 Access the Checklist tile on your CHOICE Course screen for reference information and job aids on How to Share Content.

ACTIVITY 6-8
Sharing Content with a Group

Data File
C:\093008Data\Working with Google Groups\Approved Vendors.xlsx

Before You Begin
The Elm Street House group currently has four members: Admin (owner), Student 01, Student 02, and Lydia Kim (non-domain user).

Scenario
You want to distribute a list of approved vendors to the people in the Elm Street House group. However, after doing so, one of the group members has left your organization so they no longer need to be able to access the shared document. You'll remove their access by removing them from the group.

1. As the Admin, upload and share the **Approved Vendors** file with the Elm Street House group.

    a) Sign in as the Admin and open the Drive app.
    b) Upload **C:\093008Data\Working with Google Groups\Approved Vendors** to your Drive folder.
    c) In your Drive app, select the file **Approved Vendors**.
    d) In the Drive toolbar, select [icon] to share **Approved Vendors** file.
    e) In the **Share with others** dialog box, in the **People** field, begin typing the group name *elm-street-house@<your_domain.com>* and select it from the **Suggested** list.
    f) From the **Permissions** drop-down list, select **Can view**.
    g) In the **Note** field, type *Please purchase supplies and services from approved vendors.*
    h) Select **Send**. If prompted, select **Yes**.
       A notification that the file has been shared with one group appears at the top of the window.
    i) Close the **Drive** tab.

2. Sign in as **Student 01** to verify that you can view the file due to your group membership.

    a) Sign in as Student 01 (student01@*<your_domain.com>*).
    b) From the **Apps** grid, select **Drive**.
    c) In the left navigation pane, select **Shared with Me**.

d) Display **Grid View** and observe the shared file.

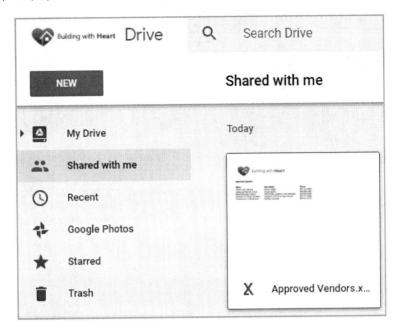

e) Sign out as Student 01.

3. Sign in as the Admin and remove **Student 01** from the member list.

   a) From the Admin console dashboard, select **Groups**.
   b) Select **Elm Street House** to open the group profile.
   c) Select **Manage users in Elm Street House** to open the **Advanced group settings** page.
   d) Select the check box next to Student 01 and then select **Remove members**.

   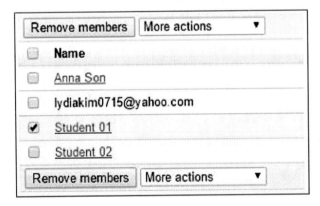

   e) Return to the Admin console.

4. Sign in as Student 01 to see if you can access the file.

   a) Sign in as **Student 01** and open Drive.
   b) Select **Shared with me** to verify that you can no longer see the shared content.
   c) Sign out as Student 01.
   d) Close the **Drive** tab.

TOPIC D

Use a Collaborative Inbox

A group mailbox provides a place for team members to communicate and work together. Instead of circulating an overwhelming amount of email messages to accomplish a task, group members can post topics to the mailbox and then assign tasks to themselves or others. Members can view the status of the assigned tasks as they move through the process.

Collaborative Inbox

A *collaborative inbox* is a type of Google Group that enables its members to work in a shared mailbox to track and manage topic posts. For example, a colleague might create a topic with a specific question about a step in the production process. All group members can see the post and the appropriate member can take on the task of responding, or assign the question to another member to handle. When responding, members have the option to respond with their personal user name or respond on behalf of the group. This type of group can be beneficial for a department that provides support to internal or external users, such as customer service or a help desk.

For administrative purposes, a collaborative inbox functions like other Google Groups. The Manage view contains the same categories in the left pane that work the same as in other groups. The email address, such as *team-inbox@domain_name.com* can be used by users to post or reply to a topic. On the group profile page, you can create an alias that is easier for users to remember and use.

The first time you open a collaborative inbox in the Groups service, you are prompted to configure the settings for how you will appear to others in this group. You can choose to hide or show your photo, link to your domain profile, and specify a display name and email address. You can also change these settings later by selecting the **My settings** button and selecting **Membership and email settings**.

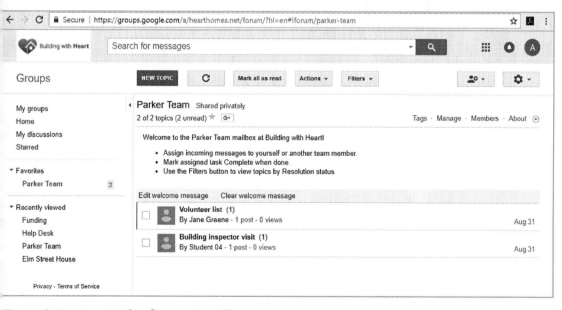

Figure 6-7: An example of a group mailbox.

Collaborative Inbox Permissions

Due to the nature of a collaborative inbox group, more settings in the Posting and Moderation categories are available to configure. As listed in the following table, more actions related to posting, replying to, and modifying topics are enabled by default. As the admin, you have the ability to configure each group mailbox differently to suit your organization's needs. For example, you might choose to make one available to non-domain users while keeping one for domain use only. Refer to Google Groups Help for detailed definitions and explanations of the permissions.

Permission Category	Enabled by Default	Disabled by Default
Basic	<ul><li>View topics</li><li>Post</li><li>Join the group</li></ul>	<ul><li>Allow members external to this organization</li><li>New member question</li></ul>
Posting	<ul><li>Add References</li><li>Assign Topics</li><li>Attach Files</li><li>Enter Free Form Tags</li><li>Mark Favorite Reply On Own Topic</li><li>Post</li><li>Post As The Group</li><li>Post Rich Text Format</li><li>Reply To Author</li></ul>	<ul><li>Have Custom Profile Photos</li><li>Me Too Topic</li><li>Post Announcements</li><li>Reply To Auto-closed Topic</li><li>Use Canned Responses</li></ul>
Moderation	<ul><li>Add Members</li><li>Approve Members</li><li>Approve Messages</li><li>Ban Users</li><li>Change Any Tag Or Category</li><li>Delete Any Post</li><li>Delete Topic</li><li>Edit Own Posts</li><li>Hide Abuse</li><li>Invite Members</li><li>Lock Topics</li><li>Mark Duplicate</li><li>Mark Favorite Reply On Any Other User's Topics</li><li>Mark No Response Needed</li><li>Modify Members</li><li>Modify Roles</li><li>Take Topic</li><li>Unassign Topic</li><li>Unmark Favorite Reply On Any Topic</li></ul>	<ul><li>Edit Others' Posts</li><li>Move Topics In</li><li>Move Topics Out</li><li>Sticky Topics</li></ul>
Access	<ul><li>Contact the owners of this Group</li><li>View Members</li><li>View Member Email Addresses</li><li>View Topics</li></ul>	N/A

Access the Checklist tile on your CHOICE Course screen for reference information and job aids on **How to Use a Collaborative Inbox.**

ACTIVITY 6-9
Creating a Collaborative Inbox for a Group

Scenario
Your team of staff and volunteers is accustomed to using email to communicate about what's happening at the Parker Street construction site. The group would appreciate having a "shared mailbox" that everyone can access to decrease the amount of messages that are sent to their individual mailboxes. Also, by creating a collaborative inbox, you can avoid the need to spend a user license for external volunteers who require only this shared communication rather than access to the entire domain.

1. As the Admin, navigate to your **Groups for Business** page and create a new group named "Parker Team."

    a) Sign in as the Admin and select ▦ to display the **Google Apps** menu. Select **Groups**. 💬
    The **Google Groups** page opens on a new browser tab.

    > **Note:** You will NOT be in the Admin console.

    b) Select the **CREATE GROUP** button.
    c) In the **Group name** field, enter *Parker Team*
    The Group email address is automatically generated based on the group name. In this case, it's parker-team@<your_domain.com>. If the name is already taken, you can append the name with a number to make it unique.
    d) In the **Group description** field, type *Shared mailbox for the Parker Street House construction site. Post questions and communicate with others here.*

2. Configure the new group type to be a **collaborative inbox** in which all members of the group can participate.

    a) From the **Select a group type** drop-down list, select **Collaborative inbox**.
    b) From the **Participants** drop-down list, verify that **All members of the group** is selected.

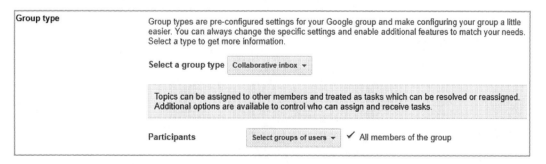

3. Configure the Basic permissions so anyone in your organization can join, view topics, and post. You also want non-domain users to be able to post and join the group by asking.

    a) From the **View topics** drop-down list, verify that **All members of the group** and **All organization members** are selected.
    b) From the **Post** drop-down list, select **Public**.

c) From the **Join the group** drop-down list, select **Anyone can ask** and verify that **Anyone in the organization** is selected.

d) Select **CREATE**.

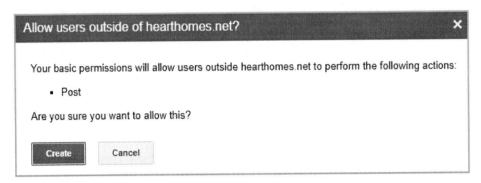

e) Select **Create** to enable users outside of your domain to post to the group.

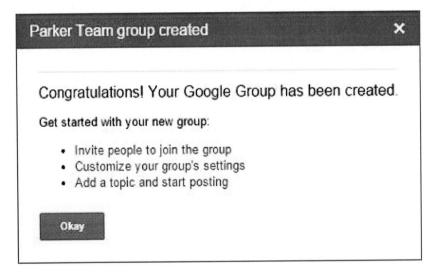

f) Select **Okay**.

4. Join the group.

a) Observe the options to change how you will look to others. Modify as you want and then select **Save my changes**.

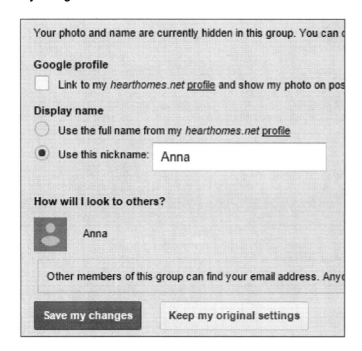

If you are not already a member, select the **Join group** button and follow the prompts to join the group. Make sure to save your changes.

b) Observe the new Parker Team topics view.
As with other Google Groups, you can add a welcome message if you want. As the Admin, you have a **Manage** button in the upper-right corner of the screen. As the creator, you were automatically added to the group.

5. Invite everyone in your organization to join the group mailbox.

   a) Select **Manage**.
   The All members list appears and you're the only member, and listed as the Owner. You could use the **Invite members** link to add users one at a time, but you want to add everyone in the organization.
   b) Switch to your Admin console dashboard and select **Groups**. Sign in as the Admin, if you aren't already.
   c) On the **Groups** page, select your newly created group mailbox, **Parker Team**.
   d) Select **Manage users in Parker Team** to open the **Advanced group settings** page.
   e) Select the **Add all users in this domain** button.

All users in *<your_domain.com>* are now listed as members of the Parker Team group.

f) Switch to the **Google Groups** tab and refresh the **Parker Team** page to verify that the entire domain has been added to the All members list.

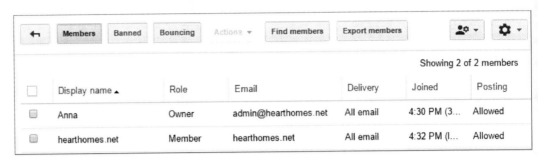

6. Sign in as Student 01 and post a topic.
   a) Use the **Account** menu to sign in as **Student 01**.
   b) From the **Google Apps** menu, select **Groups**.
      The **Google Groups** page opens on a new browser tab.
   c) On the Google Groups **Home** page, select **Browse all**.

   Parker Team appears in the group list. Student 01 was added to the Members list when everyone in <your_domain.com> was added to the Members list.
   d) Select the **Parker Team** to open the group.
   e) Select **Join group** button, edit your display name and email settings (if desired), and then select **Join this group**.
   f) Select **NEW TOPIC**, enter a Subject and content of your choice, and then select **POST**.

7. Sign in as a non-domain user and post a topic to the **Parker Team** inbox.
   a) From the **Account** menu, sign in as **Lydia Kim** or another non-domain user.
   b) Observe the Parker Team message in the **Groups for Business** window.

   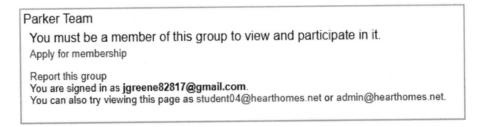

   c) From the **Google Apps** menu, open **Gmail**.
   d) Compose a new message addressed to *parker-team@hearthomes.net* with a message of your choice and then select **Send**.

8. Switch to the Admin account and view the new topics that have been posted.

9. Close the **Parker Team Google Groups** tab.

Summary

In this lesson, you learned about managing Groups for Business groups. You created, modified, and deleted groups. You explored the different interfaces that are used to manage groups: the Admin console dashboard Groups control and the Groups for Business page. You managed groups by adding and inviting members. Additionally, you used the permissions to allow and deny access to the group.

In your opinion, what advantage is there to having a Groups for Business group?

Would your organization benefit from a collaborative inbox group?

Note: Check your CHOICE Course screen for opportunities to interact with your classmates, peers, and the larger CHOICE online community about the topics covered in this course or other topics you are interested in. From the Course screen you can also access available resources for a more continuous learning experience.

7 Administering Calendars and Resources

Lesson Time: 2 hours

Lesson Introduction

Google Calendar™ and calendar resources are important tools for business people working together. In addition to being able to manage your own calendar and schedule, the ability to delegate access to another person can be a valuable backup support tool for admins. Across the domain, you can share resources, such as meeting rooms and equipment, and give users the ability to schedule a resource.

Lesson Objectives

In this lesson, you will:

- Create a group calendar that multiple users can access.
- Assign users access to calendars.
- Create meeting rooms, projectors, and other resources that can be used and scheduled in Calendar.

TOPIC A

Create and Share a Group Calendar

When groups of people work together, they often find it useful to have a shared calendar. This way, everyone in the group can see and edit calendar events for all. Additionally, you can modify the group calendar access by modifying the group.

Group Calendars

Group calendars provide a way for multiple people to view calendar events. Using the Calendar app, the same steps used to create a personal calendar are also used to create group calendars. You start in your Calendar app, and then select **Create new calendar** from the My Calendars list and fill in the basic calendar details. A group calendar is created when you share the calendar with a group email address. Of course, you could enter the individual email addresses separately; however, this can become tedious. One advantage to using a group email address is the ability to modify who has access to the calendar by editing the group membership.

Calendar Sharing Methods

There are two ways to share a group calendar. The method you choose will depend on the nature of the group and purpose of the calendar.

- Share the calendar by sending an invitation to specific users or groups. This option is commonly used to invite group members to a recently shared calendar.
- Advertise the calendar by inserting the calendar address on your website. This option is commonly used to distribute a shared calendar in training materials for new users.

Calendar Sharing Settings

The **Share this Calendar** tab contains the configuration settings necessary to share a calendar with everyone in your domain or just specific people. You can define the sharing settings when you create a new calendar. The available **Permission Settings** are the same as those used with personal calendars.

- Make changes AND manage sharing.
- Make changes to events.
- See all event details.
- See only free/busy (hide event details).

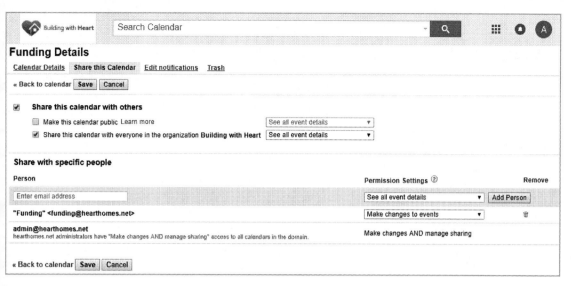

Figure 7-1: The Share this Calendar tab for a group calendar.

 Access the Checklist tile on your CHOICE Course screen for reference information and job aids on How to Create and Share a Group Calendar.

ACTIVITY 7-1
Creating and Sharing a Group Calendar

Scenario

The fund raising group at Building with Heart has requested a shared calendar to keep track of their events. You want everyone in the organization to be able to see the calendar of events. However, only the people in the Funding group should be able to create and edit the calendar events.

1. From the Admin console, create a public group named **Funding** and add two users to the group.
    a) At the Admin console, sign in with the admin credentials, if you're not already signed in.
    b) Select **Groups**.
    c) In the lower-right corner, select **Create group**.
    d) In the **Create new group** dialog box, name the group *Funding* with the Group email address of *funding@hearthomes.net*
    e) Verify that the Access Level is **Public**, but do not add all domain users to this group.
    f) Select **CREATE**.
    g) From the **Funding** group profile page, select [icon] and add **Student 01** and **Student 02** to the group.

2. Create a group calendar named **Funding**.
    a) Select [icon] and then select [icon] to open your Calendar.
    b) If this is the first time Calendar is opened, select **Got it** to close the **What's new in Google Calendar** pop-up window.
    c) In the left pane, from the **My calendars** drop-down list, select **Create new calendar**.
    d) In the **Calendar Name** field, enter *Funding*
    e) In the **Description** field, enter *Shared calendar for funding-related events.*
    f) Accept the default **Country** and **Time Zone**.

3. Share this calendar with everyone in the domain, but only the Funding group has permission to make changes to the events.
    a) Select **Share this calendar with others** and then verify that **Share this calendar with everyone in the organization Building with Heart** is selected.
    b) Verify that **See all event details** is selected to share the calendar with everyone in the domain.

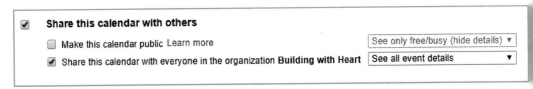

    c) Under **Share with specific people**, in the **Person** field, enter *funding@<your_domain.com>* to quickly share this calendar with everyone in the Funding group.

d) From the **Permission Settings** drop-down list, select **Make changes to events**.

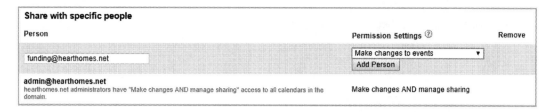

e) Select **Add Person** to add the Funding group email to the "Share with specific people" list. Only the Funding group has permission to view and change events in the shared calendar. Everyone else in your domain can view the events.
f) Select **Create Calendar**.
g) Expand **My calendars**.

The new Funding calendar appears in your **My calendars** list and is assigned a color that's different from your existing calendars.

4. Sign in as a member of the Funding group and add the shared calendar **Funding** to your calendar.
   a) Sign in as *Student 01@hearthomes.net* and open **Gmail**.
   b) Open the email from the Admin with the subject **Admin@<your_domain.com> has shared a calendar with you** and display the full message, if necessary.

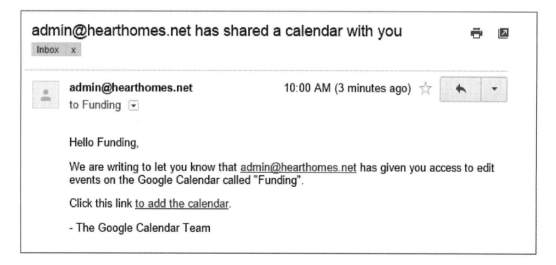

The email explains that you have been given access to edit the events.

c) Select the link **to add the calendar**.

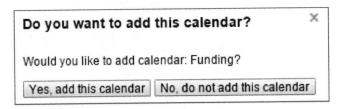

Your Calendar app opens and you are prompted to confirm adding the Funding calendar.

d) If prompted, select **Yes, add this calendar**.
e) Expand **Other calendars**.

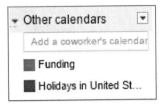

The shared calendar Funding now appears in your **Other calendars** list.

5. As a member, add an event to the Funding calendar.
   a) Select a time period on the calendar to open the **Event** dialog box.
   b) In the **What** field, enter *Charity Auction*
   c) From the **Calendar** drop-down list, select **Funding**.

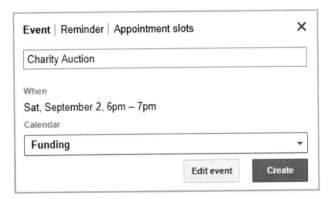

   d) Select **Create event**.

6. Switch to the Admin account, verify that the event appears.

TOPIC B

Delegate Calendar Access

Another beneficial calendar feature is the ability to give someone else access to your calendar. By delegating control of your calendar to another person, you enable them to help maintain your schedule.

Calendar Access

In general, managers give their administrative assistants the ability to work in their calendars to keep their meeting schedules organized. Or, if you're planning to be out for an extended period of time, you might want to delegate access to your calendar to someone else. The specific tasks to be handled will depend on the calendar owner/calendar delegate relationship, but might include creating and editing events, responding to meeting invitations, and managing calendar sharing. Delegating does not include changing calendar settings, modifying the contact list, or using the task list.

Access the Checklist tile on your CHOICE Course screen for reference information and job aids on How to Delegate Access to Calendars.

ACTIVITY 7-2
Delegating Access to Your Calendar

Scenario
You are planning an extended leave of absence and need to delegate access to your calendar. While the most logical choice might be to give one of the team members the responsibility, it might be better to give it to another domain admin.

1. Share your personal Admin calendar with the other Super Admin (student02@<your_domain.com>) in your domain.
    a) Sign in with your Admin credentials.
    b) Open your **Calendar**.
    c) Select the drop-down arrow next to your personal calendar.

    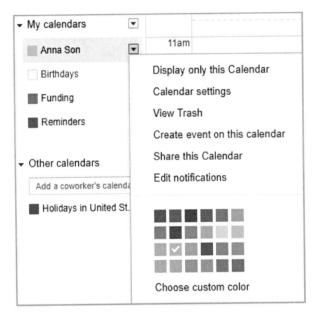

    d) Select **Share this Calendar**.
    e) In the **Share with specific people** section, in the **Person** field, type *student02@<your_domain.com>* When you select Student02@<your_domain.com> from the suggested list of names, they are automatically added to the "Share with specific people" list.
    f) Under **Permission Settings** for Student 02, verify that **Make changes AND manage sharing** is selected.

    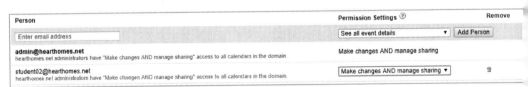

    g) Select **Save**.

2. Sign in as Student 02 and verify that you have access to the Admin's calendar.
   a) Sign in as **Student 02**.
   b) Open your Calendar, if it's not already open.
      When you switch accounts using the **Account** menu, the new account essentially "signs into" the current window, which is the Calendar.
   c) If prompted to add the Funding calendar, select **Yes, add this calendar**.
   d) In the left pane, expand **My calendars** and verify that the Admin's calendar is listed.

An email message was also sent to Student 02 telling them that they have been given access to manage events and share settings for the Admin's calendar.

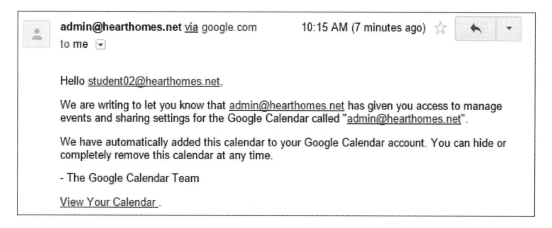

3. Sign out as Student 02.

TOPIC C

Create and Manage Calendar Resources

Many organizations have resources, such as meeting rooms or audio-visual equipment, that need to be reserved. Most likely, these resources are needed to conduct a meeting. Therefore, it makes sense for these resources to be available to schedule using the calendar.

Shared Resources

Shared resources are calendar items that are not events, but they can be scheduled. Common shared resources include meeting rooms, audio/video equipment, company cars, temporary office spaces, or lab equipment.

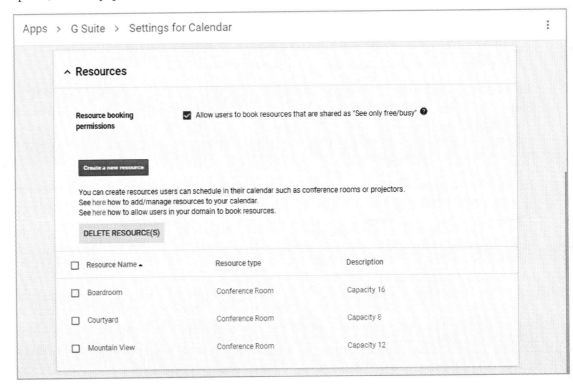

Figure 7-2: Creating shared resources.

The general steps for creating and managing shared resources include:

1. Create the resource. (It can take up to 24 hours before the resource is available for everyone.)
2. Add the resource to your calendar.
3. Share the resource.
4. Add resources to an event. (For recurring events, resource must be available for at least one-third of the events and can be unavailable for fewer than five instances only.)
5. Configure how you want to receive resource notifications.

Note about sharing permission settings: The resource must be shared as "See all event details" for users to be able to schedule it. If this setting isn't used, the resource will decline invitations to events. To limit the number of users who can add the resource to their events, you need to explicitly add them and give them one of the following permissions: **See all event details**, **Make changes to events**, or **Make changes AND sharing**. Other users will be able to see the resource, but they will not be able to reserve it.

Resource Naming Conventions

You need to create naming conventions so users can easily find the shared resources. Some guidelines might include:

- When shared resources can be seen by users in multiple locations, include a city, state, or country identifier.
- Use one naming convention for rooms and another for non-rooms so they appear differently in the resource picker list.
- Use a standard format, or syntax, to help users easily identify the resource they need.
- Use a dash character to separate different levels of the resource hierarchy. When more than 10 resources appear, they are listed as a hierarchy (such as folders and sub-folders).

Resource Notifications

You can receive email or text message notifications when a resource is added to a new event, a scheduled event is changed or canceled, or a reply to an event is received. You can also receive a daily schedule for resources. You can also assign a resource manager that acts as a gatekeeper and has the ability to approve or reject the scheduling requests for a particular resource.

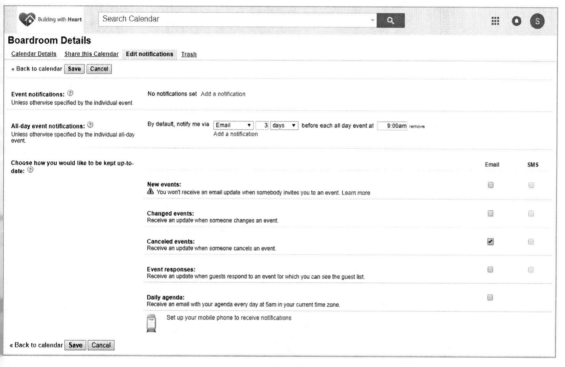

Figure 7-3: Editing the notification settings for a resource.

Access the Checklist tile on your CHOICE Course screen for reference information and job aids on How to Manage Shared Resources.

ACTIVITY 7-3
Creating Shared Resources

Scenario
Your organization has three conference rooms that can be used for meetings and other events. Because each room has different maximum seating, you want to include the capacity so people book the appropriate room. The room names and capacity are:

- Boardroom—Capacity: 16
- Courtyard—Capacity: 8
- Mountain View—Capacity: 12

1. Create a shared resource.
   a) Sign in to the Admin console as Admin, if you aren't already signed in.
   b) From the Admin console, select **Apps→G Suite→Calendar** to configure **Calendar** settings.
   c) Select **Resources** to expand the **Resources** section.
      Your shared resources will appear here.
   d) Select the **Create a new resource** button.
   e) In the **Resource name** field, enter *Boardroom*
   f) In the **Resource type** field, enter *Conference Room*
   g) In the **Description** field, enter *Capacity 16*
   h) Select **SAVE**.

2. Add the **Courtyard** and **Mountain View** conference rooms, including the **Capacity** in the description.

3. Be sure to select **SAVE** and then compare your **Resources** section to the following image.

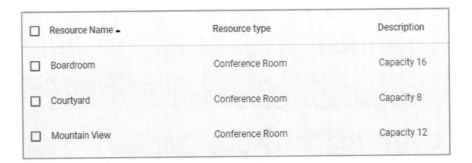

 Note: After creating the resources, it might take up to 24 hours before the resources are available to everyone.

4. Switch to your Admin calendar and add the new resources by subscribing to them.
   a) From your calendar, select the drop-down arrow next to **Other calendars** and select **Browse Interesting Calendars**.

You can subscribe to different holidays, favorite sports teams, and more.
b) Select the **More** tab.
c) Select **Resources for** *<your_domain.com>* to display the list of shared resources you just created.

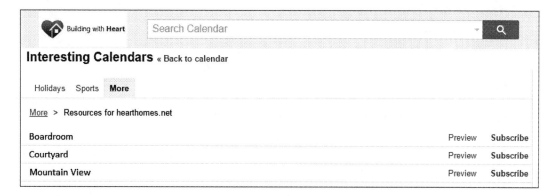

d) For the **Boardroom**, **Courtyard**, and **Mountain View** resources, select **Subscribe**.
e) At the top of the page, select the **Back to calendar** link and observe that the resources have been added to your **My calendars** list.

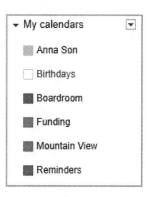

Because you created the shared resources, they appear in your **My calendars** list. For others, the shared resources appear in their **Other calendars** list.

5. Add the shared resource to an event.
   a) From your calendar, create a new *Volunteer Meeting* event.
   b) Select the **Edit Event** button.

c) Select **Rooms** to display the available rooms.

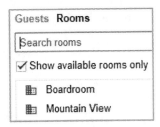

d) Select **Boardroom** to add the room to the **Where** field and the **Participants** list.

You can select the **x** to remove a resource just as you would remove a guest.

e) Select **SAVE**.

6. Observe the newly added Volunteer Meeting on your calendar.

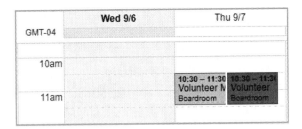

You will see two separate entries on your calendar because the shared resources are also displayed on your calendar. You can hide the shared resources by displaying the shortcut menu for the resource you want to hide, and then selecting **Hide this calendar from the list**. The resource will still be available for you to schedule; it just won't be displayed on your calendar.

 Note: If you want to display the resource calendars again, from the **My calendars** drop-down menu, select **Settings**. In the **SHOW IN LIST** column, select the calendar(s) to be displayed. This is also another way to hide the shared resources from your calendar.

Resource Manager

By default, shared resources automatically accept invitations to events that do not have conflicts. You might want to have tighter control of the shared resources by assigning a person to act as a gatekeeper. Known as a *resource manager*, he or she would handle all incoming requests for a particular resource by accepting or declining on behalf of the resource.

To set up a resource manager, you will need to modify the **Auto-accept invitations** setting to **Automatically add all invitations to this calendar**. Then, once you identify the person taking on this role, you need to explicitly share the resource with them. Be sure to give them the **Make changes AND manage sharing** permissions for the shared resource.

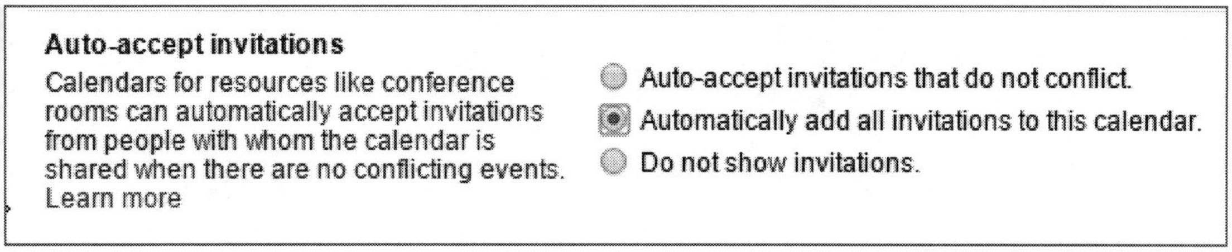

Auto-accept invitations

Calendars for resources like conference rooms can automatically accept invitations from people with whom the calendar is shared when there are no conflicting events. Learn more

○ Auto-accept invitations that do not conflict.
◉ Automatically add all invitations to this calendar.
○ Do not show invitations.

Figure 7-4: Configuring a resource manager.

Access the Checklist tile on your CHOICE Course screen for reference information and job aids on **How to Configure a Resource Manager.**

ACTIVITY 7-4
Setting Up a Resource Manager

Before You Begin
You have created three conference rooms.

Scenario
Unlike the user's calendar, the shared resources at Building with Heart are not monitored by any one person. This can create problems if two people want to use the Boardroom at the same time. Rather than have this resource be scheduled on a first-come-first-served basis, you want someone to make priority calls when scheduling conflicts arise. It's very important for the Boardroom to be available for those critical donor meetings. Naturally, plans and schedules change, but knowing before an all-day event is scheduled to occur would be very helpful. Student 02 has agreed to be the resource monitor and has decided that receiving an email with the daily agenda would be a great asset.

1. Open the **Calendars Settings** page.
    a) Verify that the Calendar is open and displayed.
    b) From the **My calendars** drop-down menu, select **Settings**. (You can also select ⚙ and then **Settings**.)
    c) On the **Calendars** tab, observe the contents of the **My calendars** section.

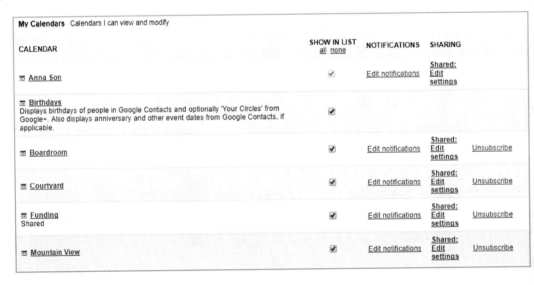

   You can configure the selected resources to show or hide them, edit notifications, modify sharing settings, and unsubscribe.
    d) Select **Back to calendar**.

2. Identify **Student02** as the resource manager for the shared **Boardroom** resource.

a) From the **My calendars** list, select the drop-down arrow next to **Boardroom**, and then select **Calendar settings** to open the **Calendar Details** tab of the Boardroom calendar.

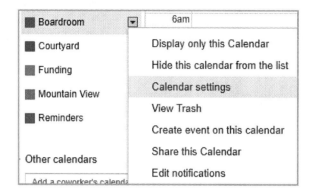

b) In the **Auto-accept invitations** section, select **Automatically add all invitations to this calendar**.
c) Select **Save**.
   The **Boardroom Details** page is closed and you are returned to your Calendar.
d) From the **Boardroom** drop-down menu, select **Share this Calendar**.
e) Verify that **Share this calendar with others** is selected and everyone in the organization has permission to **See all event details**.

f) In the **Person** field, enter *Student02@<your_domain.com>* and verify that in the **Permission Settings**, **Make changes AND manage sharing** is selected.

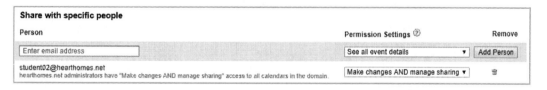

You can modify the permission settings at a later time, as well as remove the person by selecting the trash can icon in the **Remove** column.
g) Select **Save**.

3. As **Student02**, edit the notifications for how you want to receive emails.
   a) From the Calendar, sign in as **Student 02**, and enter your password.
   b) From the **Boardroom** drop-down menu, select **Edit notifications** to open the **Edit notifications** tab.
   c) In the **All-day event notifications** section, select **Add a notification**.
   d) Configure the notification to send an **Email 3 days before the scheduled event**.

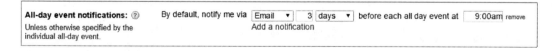

   e) Select the **Email** check box for **Canceled events** as your method for keeping up-to-date.
   f) Select **Save**.

4. Switch between the Admin and Student 02 (resource manager) to trigger and view email notifications.

a) Sign in as the **Admin** and reserve the **Boardroom** for an all-day meeting with your top five donors.
b) Sign in as **Student 02** and open **Gmail**.
Because the event is more than 3 days away, you didn't receive an email notification. However, the event appears on your Boardroom calendar.
c) As the **Admin**, select the Top 5 Donor event and select **Delete** to cancel the meeting.

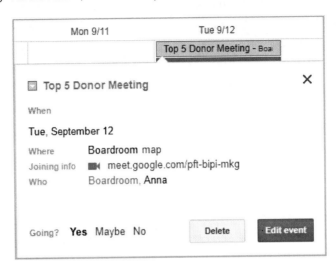

d) As **Student 02**, open the **Canceled Event** email to view the event cancellation notice.

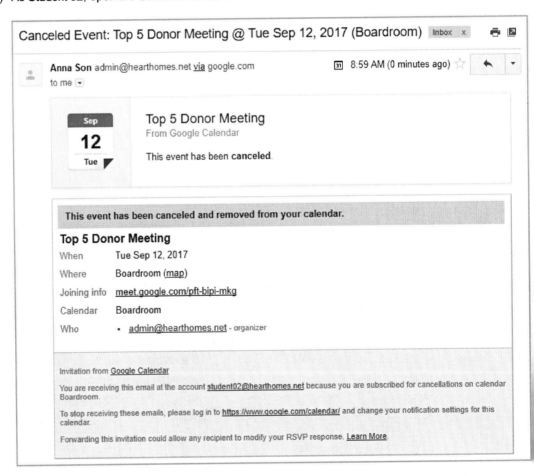

The links at the bottom of the email can be used to stop subscribing to cancellations as well as to modify the other notification settings.

e) Sign out as Student 02.

5. Close all open **Calendar** tabs, and return to the Admin console **Home** page.

Summary

In this lesson, you learned about creating shared calendars to help a group stay organized. You also gave another person access to your calendar to help you manage your schedule. Finally, you created shared resources, such as conference rooms, and assigned someone to be the resource manager.

Can you think of instances when having a resource manager would be beneficial?

Do the shared calendar resources in your organization appear available for everyone or are they restricted for selected people?

Note: Check your CHOICE Course screen for opportunities to interact with your classmates, peers, and the larger CHOICE online community about the topics covered in this course or other topics you are interested in. From the Course screen you can also access available resources for a more continuous learning experience.

8 | Configuring and Securing Mobile Devices

Lesson Time: 1 hour

Lesson Introduction

As the admin, you can control who has the ability to use a mobile device to access the G Suite account email and data. You also want to make sure all devices have strong passwords to protect them and the domain if they are lost or stolen. Defining a Google Apps Device Policy and enforcing it is a good start toward protecting your domain. Additionally, the policy can be designed to give you the ability to remotely manage the devices.

Lesson Objectives

In this lesson, you will:

- Enable users to access the domain with a mobile device.
- Manage users' mobile devices.

TOPIC A

Set Up Google Mobile Management

There's a high probability that users will want to use their smartphones or tablets to access and work with their G Suite accounts. As the administrator, this can be a nightmare to manage when users are using their personal devices with company data. Your first line of defense is having the ability to allow or deny specific devices access to your domain.

Device Management

You can use the **Device management** control on the Admin console dashboard to set network, mobile, and Chrome settings in your G Suite domain. This allows you to manage Chrome devices, mobile devices such as Android and iOS, enforce security policies, and control the available apps and services. The process to configure mobile devices will depend on the types of settings and devices being used. Apple® iOS® and Android™ devices require a specialized setup.

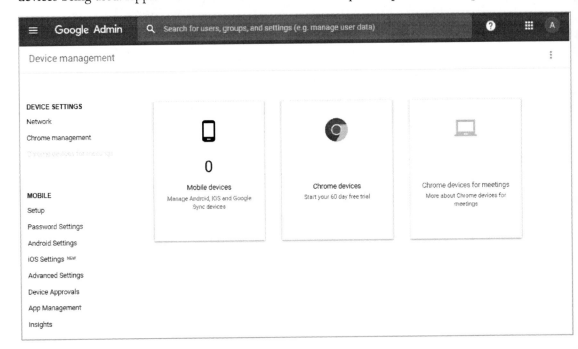

Figure 8-1: The Device management page.

From the **Device management** page, you can select the **Mobile devices** box to display the list of mobile devices.

Figure 8-2: Mobile devices page.

Supported Devices

The following mobile devices are supported by Google to communicate with your G Suite domain:

- Android
- Apple iOS (iOS 7 is no longer supported in G Suite Basic)
- Google Sync™ devices
  - Windows Phone®
  - BlackBerry® 10
  - Smartphones and tablets using Microsoft® Exchange ActiveSync
- Chrome™ devices
- Chromebox™

Chrome Devices

A Chrome device is a laptop or other physical device designed to run the Chrome operating system. Chrome devices are designed to take advantage of cloud storage and how people work today. A *Chromebook™* is a laptop with a reduced amount of RAM and a smaller hard drive that tends to be lighter in weight and cheaper in cost compared to standard Windows-based laptops. With a purchase of a Chromebook, users are given 100 GB of free storage for two years. Each Chromebook comes with Chrome and the other common productivity apps so your initial setup can be as easy as signing in to your Google account. G Suite account users might have a Chromebook as their only computer, or use one in combination with another laptop or mobile device.

A *Chromebox* is a physical device that can be easily connected to a monitor for conducting video conference meetings. The Chromebox kit contains the necessary cables needed to attach an external HDMI monitor, a speaker with microphone, a web camera, and a remote control used to run all of the attached devices. By using your G Suite account, you can sign in to the account and complete the setup process. Once connected, you can link the Chromebox device to a room in your account. The Chromebox uses Google Hangouts™ as the meeting interface. The Hangouts Plugin for Microsoft Outlook® enables organizations without a G Suite account to conduct video calls through Outlook.

 Note: The Chromebook was designed to be a simple, inexpensive laptop for organizations, especially educational institutions.

Chrome Device Management

You can use the Admin console dashboard **Device Management→Chrome Devices** to manage the following:

- User settings on Chrome browsers and Chrome devices
- Public session settings on Chrome devices
- Chrome devices
- Chrome apps

By default, Chrome devices are added to the top-level organization. However, like user accounts, the Chrome devices can be moved to an organizational unit and managed as a collective group. As part of an organizational unit, the Chrome devices are controlled by the same access privileges as the users in that organizational unit.

When adding, known as deploying, Chrome devices to your domain, there are five general steps to follow. (You can refer to the Chrome Device Deployment Guide for more details.)

1. Verify that your site can handle the bandwidth. Google recommends 30 devices per access point.
2. From the Admin console, configure the Wi-Fi network settings.
3. Configure the Chrome device policies.
4. Enroll one Chrome device as a test.
5. If the test is successful, enroll and deploy the other devices.

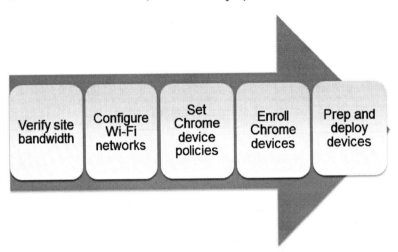

Figure 8-3: Deploying Chrome devices in your domain.

 Note: To learn more about Chrome devices in a domain, check out the LearnTO **Enroll Chrome Devices** presentation from the **LearnTO** tile on the CHOICE Course screen.

Chrome Device Policies

An administrator can set Chrome device policies to control how Chrome devices behave, regardless of which user is logged in. This can be very useful if you want Chrome to behave the same way on shared devices, or on devices where the user has logged in as guest.

As you set different policies, you can choose which organization or sub organization to apply the policies to. In this way, you can manage settings at the domain or organizational unit (sub organization) level.

Chrome device policies include the following settings.

Policy Area	Description
Enrollment and Access	Use to force re-enrollment, verify device identity, and provide instructions for returning disabled devices to the organization.
Sign-in Settings	Restrict who can sign in, including Guest, complete domain name, display username and photo on sign in screen, erase user info after sign out, control single sign on cookies, and accessibility settings.
Device Update Settings	Control device updates.
Kiosk Settings	Control shared devices.
User and Device Reporting	Control reporting on the device.
Power and Shutdown	Control power management, shutdowns, and reboots.
Other	Control cloud-based printing, time zone settings, and mobile data roaming.

Note: Chrome device policy settings are not available until your organization actually buys a Chrome device (Chrome device license).

Chrome User Settings

An administrator can set Chrome User Settings, also known as Chrome policies, specifically for users who use the Chrome browser or Chrome devices. The settings, however, are applied to the user, not the device itself. As with device settings and policies, user settings and policies can be different for each sub organization. Depending on how you apply the policy, one user might get one group of settings, then another user might get another group of settings. Chrome user policies are managed in the cloud, so they are applied when the users signs in, regardless if the devices are public or private. Since Chrome user policies are applied to user accounts in your organization, they will not apply if the user signs in as Guest, or if the user signs into a Google account outside of your organization, such as a personal Gmail account.

Chrome user policies include the following settings.

Policy Area	Description
Mobile	Choose if policies should apply to the Chrome browser on mobile devices.
General	Set custom wallpaper, avatars, and Smart Lock.
Enrollment Controls	Manage device enrollment, asset identification, and enrollment permissions.
Apps and Extensions	Allow or block different types of apps and extensions, including Chrome Web Store home page and permissions settings. Also force install apps and extensions directly to students using Google Play for Education.
Chrome Web Store	Customize the homepage and web store permissions.
Android applications	Allow users to install Android-specific applications on their Chrome devices.
Security	Manage passwords, screenlocks, safe browser settings, geolocation settings, single sign on, malicious site blocking, and minimum SSL version.
Session Settings	Display the Logout button in the system tray for easier use.
Network	Set proxy and advanced SSL security settings.

Policy Area	Description
Startup	Set home page, add home button, and choose which pages to load on startup.
Content	Control cookies, JavaScript, plugins, client certificates, URL blacklisting, and Google Drive sync settings.
Printing	Manage printing.
User Experience	Manage bookmarks, download location, pre-fill, multiple sign in, Google translate, and Unified Desktop.
Omnibox Search Provider	Manage search settings.
Hardware	Manage audio, video, keyboard, and external storage devices.

Access the Checklist tile on your CHOICE Course screen for reference information and job aids on **How to Configure Chrome User and Device Policies.**

Google Mobile Management

In addition to Chrome devices, Google Mobile Management helps you manage settings and enforce security policies on mobile devices in your G Suite domain. These devices include Android, Apple iOS, Windows Phones, and BlackBerry 10. You can apply policies to the top-level organization or to a selected organizational unit. By assigning users to organizational units, you can create customized device policies for each organizational unit. If devices are syncing with multiple G Suite domains, the most restrictive policy will be enforced.

Many of the security settings are available for many versions of Android and iOS devices. However, there are a limited number of settings that are available only for a specific device. The following tables provide a summary of the available security settings that can be configured and enforced on all devices, only Android devices, or only iOS devices. For additional information and details, refer to the G Suite Administrator Help.

Note: If you have a variety of Android devices (versions 2.2 through 3.0 and higher), then do not enable both **Enforce policies on Android devices** and **Encrypt data on device**. Doing so will prevent Android 2.3 and earlier devices from being able to synchronize their G Suite data.

Setting	Description	Available for
Enable Sync for users	Enables sync between the device and the G Suite account.	All devices
Enforce policies	Enforces policies on devices.	All devices
Allow Google Glass	Enables Google Glass to access domain accounts.	Google Glass
Password	Requires users to set a password and defines password settings, including password strength, minimum length, number of days before expiration, number of expired passwords that are blocked, automatic lock time, and number of invalid passwords before device is wiped.	All devices
Device Setup	Enable Device Owner option during initial device setup	All devices

Setting	Description	Available for
Device settings	• Encrypt data on the device. • Allow automatic sync when roaming. • Allow camera.	All devices
Advanced settings	• Enable application auditing. • Allow user to remote wipe device. • Enable device activation.	All devices
Google Play	Controls what apps users can add to their devices.	All devices
Google Play Private Apps	Allows users to access and update Google Play private apps—a feature of the Google Play Store which lets you distribute Android apps internally to users in your G Suite domain.	All devices
Google Sync	Defines an IP whitelist for Google Sync access, as well as automatically enables the **Delete Email to Trash** setting on Google Sync devices.	All devices
Google Now™	Enables Google Now intelligent personal assistant developed by Google.	Android, iOS, Google Chrome web browser on personal computers
Unknown Sources	Disables install from unknown sources.	All devices
Developer Options	Allows users to enable developer options.	All devices
VPN (Virtual Private Network)	Allows users to configure VPN settings.	All devices
Verify Apps	Allows users to disable application verification.	All devices
Mobile Networks	Allow users to configure mobile network settings.	All devices
Trusted Credentials	Allow users to view and modify device certificates.	All devices
Apps Settings	Allow users to modify installed applications.	All devices
Physical Media	Allows users to use external SD cards on their devices.	All devices
Microphone Volume	Allows users to adjust the microphone volume on their devices.	All devices
Speaker Volume	Allows users to adjust the device speakers.	All devices
Screen Capture	Allows screen capturing.	All devices
Notification	Allows notification details for locked devices.	All devices
Account Addition	Allows addition of Google Accounts.	All devices
Add Users	Allows users to add new users on their devices.	All devices

Setting	Description	Available for
Remove Users	Allows users to remove users from their devices.	All devices
Cell Broadcasts	Allow users to configure cell broadcast settings.	All devices
Tethering	Allows users to configure tethering and portable hotspot settings.	All devices
Factory Reset	Allows users to factory reset their devices.	All devices
Factory Reset Protection Setting	Accounts that can be used to access the device after a factory reset.	All devices
Administrator Restriction PIN settings	Enables remote management of administrator restriction PIN.	All devices

Android and Android for Work Settings

The following settings are available for only Android or Android for Work devices.

Setting	Description
Lock screen widgets	(Android only) Enables lock screen widgets.
Auto account wipe	(Android only) Enables automatic wipe if device doesn't sync and defines number of days device can go without syncing.
Compromised device	(Android only) Blocks compromised devices.
Enforce Work Profile	Requires Android for Work users (Android 5.0+) to create a work profile that keeps work and personal accounts separate.
Sharing to other profiles	Enables sharing from Work Profile to Personal Space.
Cross Profile Copy Paste	Allows copy and paste from Work Profile to Personal space.
Primary lockdown settings	Allows users to share location information with apps and add or remove accounts.
USB file transfer	Enable USB file transfer.

iOS Only Settings

The following settings are available only on iOS devices.

Setting	Description
Lock Screen	
• Control Center	Allows control center on lock screen.
• Notification view	Allows notification view on lock screen.
• Today view	Allows Today view on lock screen.
Managed Apps	Settings to control and manage apps that users install on iOS devices through the Google Device Policy.
Account Configurations	
• CalDav	Enables calendar sync.
• CardDav	Enables contact sync.
Backup and iCloud Sync	

Setting	Description
• iCloud backup	Allows backing up to iCloud.
• Encrypted backup	Forces backup encryption on iOS.
• Document sync	Allows document and key-value syncing to iCloud.
• Keychain sync	Allows keychain syncing to iCloud.
Safari	Settings to manage iOS web browsing, such as the Autofill feature, secure browsing warnings, JavaScript, pop-ups, and cookies.
Photos	Settings to manage how photos on the device's camera are synced with iCloud Photo Library and iCloud Photo Sharing.
Advanced Security	Settings to control the screen capture feature, Siri, Apple Watch, and Apple Handoff.

Apple Push Certificate for iOS Devices

As the admin of the G Suite domain, you need to configure the device management settings for iOS devices so they can connect to your domain and sync their data. By default, the sync on mobile setting is enabled for all devices, including iOS devices.

Before you can configure the advanced mobile management settings, Google requires you to download and configure an **Apple Push Certificate**. There are multiple steps which require sending a certificate request (google_ios_push_certificate.csr file) and receiving a signed certificate (MDM_Google Inc. (Ent)_Certificate.pem) in return from Google.

After the Apple Push Certificate is set up, users will be able to connect to their G Suite domain. The first time that they connect to the G Suite domain, they will be prompted to install a Google Device Policy.

You can view the details of your Apple Push Certificate and renew it, when necessary, by selecting the **Device management** control from the Admin console. On the left, under **Mobile**, select **Setup→Apple Push Certificate**.

Figure 8-4: The Apple Push Certificates Portal.

Android for Work Devices

Android for Work devices are mobile devices with Android 5.0+ and support Work Profiles, which are used to separate the user's work accounts and data from their personal accounts and data on the same device. While it's beneficial to have control over mobile devices that access your G Suite domain, you do not want to adversely affect a user's personal apps and data, especially if they own the device. Android Work Profiles provide the ability to manage the work-related accounts on devices without harming any personal data.

You can manage these devices by using the **Android Settings→Work Profile** settings on the **Device management** page. However, you will need to authorize Google to be your Enterprise Mobility Management (EMM) provider. This is done by generating a token that you then enter on the **Mobile management** profile in the **Android Settings→Work Profile** section.

Google Sync

Google Sync is the service that uses Microsoft Exchange ActiveSync to synchronize mail, calendar, and contacts between G Suite accounts and mobile devices. By default, this feature is enabled for users and the synchronization happens behind the scenes. However, as the admin, you can disable the feature as well as fine-tune the configuration settings to enforce security on mobile devices. Google Sync works with iOS, Windows Phone, Windows Mobile, and BlackBerry 10 devices. Android devices do not require Google Sync because synchronization with Google is built in to the device.

Note: Previously, this service was available to anyone with a personal Google account, but as of January 30, 2013, it's now only available to G Suite, Government, and Education accounts.

Mobile Device Setup

When setting up mobile device management in your domain, you have the option to work through a step-by-step setup process or use the automatic setup. Regardless of the setup method you choose, you can modify the settings later.

In addition to the two setup methods, there are four major management options:

- **Basic management:** Provides users with basic connection to G Suite and provides you with the ability to enforce screen locks and passcodes, wipe corporate data, view devices, and export device details.
- **Advanced management:** Provides all the basic features plus the ability to manage business apps, approve services before being synced, use encryption, and apply organizational unit policies. Additionally, you have a centralized location for viewing and managing the mobile devices as well as accessing reports, audits, and alerts.
- **Custom management:** Enables you to specify advanced settings for Android, iOS, and Google Sync devices.
- **No management:** Gives users the ability to sync their G Suite data with their devices without giving the admin the ability to apply policies or manage the devices.

Access the Checklist tile on your CHOICE Course screen for reference information and job aids on How to Set Up Mobile Device Management.

ACTIVITY 8-1
Setting Up Device Management

Scenario
Building with Heart has recently been gifted with new Android tablets for staff and volunteers to use. As the admin, you need to enable these mobile devices so your staff and the external volunteers are able to access their G Suite account mail and other shared resources.

Some staff members also use the Chrome browser on their Windows laptops to access email. Recently, there have been a number of incidents in which users' laptops have become infected by malicious sites. You would like to set a Chrome policy to protect users from accidentally visiting these sites.

1. From the Admin console dashboard, enable users to access and sync with their G Suite domain accounts.
   a) Sign in as the Admin.
   b) From the Admin console dashboard, select ▢ to open the **Device management** page.
   c) Under **MOBILE**, select **Setup** to open the **Setup** profile.

   d) Select **Mobile Management**.

2. Configure the **Setup** settings to enable syncing from mobile devices for users.

a) In the **Organizations** section, ensure that **hearthomes.net** has been selected.

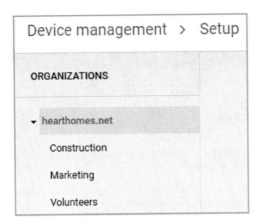

By default, the top-level organization is selected and the sub organizations will inherit these settings. However, you can select the sub organizations and configure their settings individually, if desired.

b) In the **Enable Mobile Management** section, select **Enabled**.

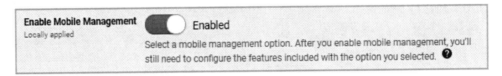

c) Select **Custom**.

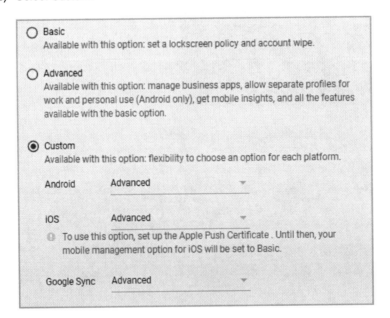

d) Select **SAVE**.
e) Select the **Device Activation** section and check **Require admin approval for device activation**.
f) Select **SAVE**.

g) In the **Sync on Mobile** section, verify that the sync is allowed for Android, iOS, and Google Sync.

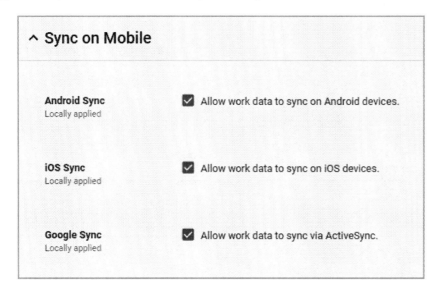

3. Protect your Chrome users from proceeding to malicious sites.
    a) On the **Device management** page, under **DEVICE SETTINGS**, select **Chrome management**.
    b) On the **Chrome Management** page, select **User settings**.
    c) Scroll down to the **Security→Malicious Sites** section.
    d) In the **Malicious Sites** drop-down box, select **Prevent user from proceeding anyway to malicious sites**.
    e) Select **SAVE**.

Mobile Device Activation

After configuring the G Suite domain to allow mobile devices, the mobile device needs to be configured to access the domain. The necessary steps will vary depending on the mobile device you have.

For **Android or Google devices**, you will need to download and install the Google Apps Device Policy app from the Google Play™ Store. Follow the steps to register the device and activate the device administrator. In other words, essentially give the G Suite domain permission to control the mobile device.

Using an **iOS device**, the first time a user tries to access their G Suite domain account, they are prompted to install the Google Apps Device Policy Profile. Users can follow the prompts to do so. They will be warned about giving the G Suite admin complete control of the device and about trusting the profile's source to remotely manage the device management. At several points, users can cancel out of the installation if they want. The installed Google Apps Device Policy Profile can be viewed in the **Settings** app and removed at any time.

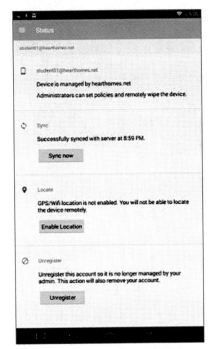

Installing Google Apps Device Policy Profile on iOS device

Status of a registered Android device

Figure 8-5: Activating a mobile device.

 Access the Checklist tile on your CHOICE Course screen for reference information and job aids on How to Activate Mobile Devices.

ACTIVITY 8-2
Activating Android Devices (Optional)

Before You Begin
You have an Android mobile device that you can use to download and install the Google Apps Device Policy app.

Scenario
Now that you've enabled users to access their G Suite accounts from a mobile device, you're being swamped with requests to help people activate their mobile device. Sam is using an older Android 4.4 tablet and needs your help to activate it and connect to his G Suite files.

---

1. Power on the device and enter the password, if prompted by the device.

2. Select the **Google Play Store** icon to open the online store.

3. Search for the Google Apps Device Policy app.

4. Download and install the Google Apps Device Policy app.
   a) Open the new policy app and walk through the guided steps to register the device.
   b) When prompted to activate the device administrator, select **Activate**.
   c) When prompted to confirm the administrator's enforcement of the policy, select **Enforce**.

5. Switch to the Admin console to approve the activated devices.
   a) From the Admin console, select **Device management→Mobile devices**.
   b) In the **Mobile devices** list, select the device you want to approve.
   c) Select the **APPROVE** button.

TOPIC B

Secure Mobile Devices

After enabling mobile devices to access your G Suite domain, you can create a security policy that controls what apps and services are available to be used on the mobile device. The ability to remotely manage a device is a powerful tool for admins.

Mobile Device Security

Mobile device security settings are an integral part of Google's device management. Most security settings can be found under **Device Management→Mobile**. Settings include:

- Policy enforcement
- Password settings
- Encryption requirements
- Auto account wipe
- Compromised device settings
- Lockdown settings
- VPN settings
- Administrator Restriction PIN
- Block and remote wipe
- Certificates

Note: You can only allow users to remotely wipe Android devices. To do so, they will have to download the Google Device Policy app from Google Play, and then register their device with your organization. They will then have to open the Android Device Manager web page at https://www.google.com/android/devicemanager?u=0 to manage their device. Currently, iOS devices do not have remote wipe capability.

Exception Groups

Ordinarily, you would use sub organizations to apply different policies, including security settings, to different users. However, there may be times when you would want to leave a user in a particular organization, but exempt that person from the policy applied to that organization. You can use exception groups to make these exemptions while leaving the user in the existing organization. Examples of users who can benefit are department managers, executives, IT administrators, or test groups.

Exception groups are regular administrator-created groups used for exception purposes. You create a group, add the desired users to it, choose the security policy that you want to exempt the group members from, and then select the group in that policy's **Group Filters** section.

Note: Currently, only advanced security settings can have exception groups. The advanced security settings are found by selecting a hyperlink under the **Basic settings** section of **Security**. Other policy settings, such as mobile device management settings, are applied at the organization and organizational unit level without exception.

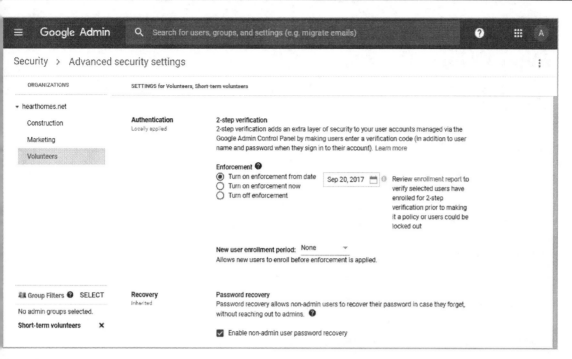

Figure 8-6: Exception Groups.

 Access the Checklist tile on your CHOICE Course screen for reference information and job aids on **How to Use Security Policies.**

ACTIVITY 8-3
Applying Security Policies

Scenario
Now that the mobile devices are able to connect to the Building with Heart domain, your domain can be vulnerable if anyone loses their device. You can protect the domain by requiring passwords on all devices and enforcing this policy. You also want to require two-factor authentication in the near future for volunteers. However, you often have short-term volunteers who only work for a few hours on special projects. To make it easier for these people to join your work force, you will exempt them from two-factor authentication.

1. Configure the device policy settings to require a password with a minimum length of 10 characters.
    a) From the Admin console, select **Device management**.
    b) Under **MOBILE**, select **Password settings**.
    c) Verify that the top-level organization is selected.
    d) In the **Password Policies** section, select **Require users to set a password**.
    e) In the **Minimum number of characters** box, enter **10**
    f) From the **Automatically lock the device after** drop-down list, select **15 minutes**.
    g) Observe the option to automatically wipe the device after a specified number of invalid passwords.

    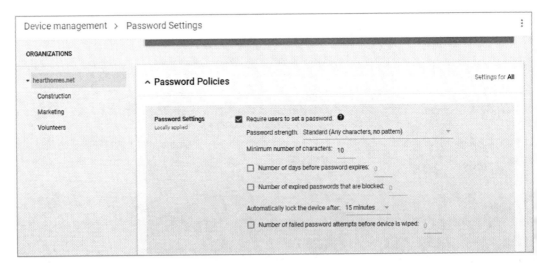

    The password settings take effect as soon as you save them. If anyone is using their device without a password, they will be prompted to enter a password with at least 10 characters the next time they sign in.
    h) Select **SAVE**.

2. Configure the device policy to allow users to remote wipe their devices.
    a) Under **Device management**, under **MOBILE**, select **Android Settings**.
    b) Select **General settings**.

c) Select **Allow users to wipe their devices from Find My Device**.

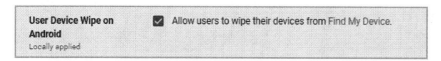

d) Observe the other available settings.
e) Select **SAVE**.

3. Create an exception group to exempt short term volunteers from two-factor authentication settings.
   a) In the Admin console, create a group called *Short-Term Volunteers* with the email address of *short-term-volunteers@<yourdomain>* and an **Access Level** of **Public**.

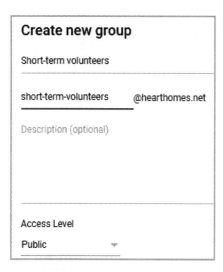

   b) Select **CREATE**.
   c) Switch to the **Security** section of the Admin console.
   d) Select **Basic settings**.
   e) In the **Two-step verification** section, ensure that **Allow users to turn on 2-step verification** is selected.

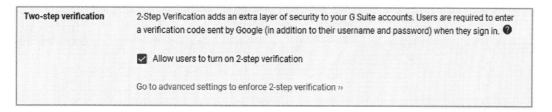

   f) Select the **Go to advanced settings to enforce 2-step verification** hyperlink. If prompted to navigate away from the page, select **OK**.
   g) In the upper left, select the **Volunteers** sub organization.
   h) In the **Authentication** section, under **Enforcement**, select the **Turn on enforcement from date** radio button.

i) Select the calendar, and choose a date in the future, after this class is expected to end.

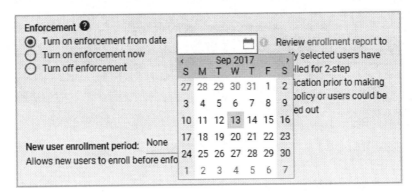

j) In the lower left, in the **Group filters** section, select **SELECT**.
k) In the **Select a group to apply filter** page, select **Short-Term Volunteers**.

 Note: If the group does not appear in the list, type the group name and then select **SEARCH**. When asked, select **Leave** and sign in with the admin credentials. Now, the new exception group should be displayed.

l) Select **DONE**.
m) Verify that **Short-Term Volunteers** now appears as an exempt group.

n) Select **SAVE**.

Export a Device List

From your Mobile devices list, you can export the device details in a CSV file. You can choose to export selected devices or all devices. Depending on the number of registered devices in your domain, this export might take some time. The exported list will be downloaded as a zip, or compressed, file to your standard **Downloads** folder. This exported list can be a useful tool for tracking devices, troubleshooting issues with devices, and managing the devices that users have synced with their domain accounts.

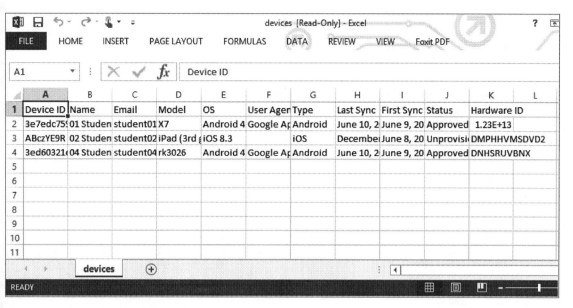

Figure 8-7: An exported device list.

Remote Wipe

The *Remote Wipe* feature deletes all content (apps and data) on a device including the SD card and returns the device to the default settings. If a device is lost or stolen, you can wipe it to protect your G Suite domain and any sensitive or confidential data from unauthorized users. Although the Remote Wipe feature erases data on the device, the data remains on the website and is accessible from a web browser or another device.

From the **Mobile devices** page, you can select the device to be erased and then select the **Remote Wipe** button. You are asked to confirm the wipe.

Wipe Account

Similar to remotely wiping a device, you can choose to erase the entire G Suite account. In addition to removing the apps and data, the *Wipe Account* feature also removes the user's G Suite account information. Unlike the Remote Wipe feature, this feature leaves the user's personal settings on the device intact. Only the G Suite account information is removed. This feature is useful when a person leaves the organization and takes their mobile device with them.

 Access the Checklist tile on your CHOICE Course screen for reference information and job aids on How to Manage Devices.

ACTIVITY 8-4
Managing Mobile Devices (Optional)

Before You Begin
You have approved mobile devices in your domain.

Scenario
After handing out the newly acquired Android tablets, you've discovered that some of the staff did not receive one. You want to make sure that all of the company devices have registered and installed the Google Device Policy app. Additionally, your major donor recruiter, Luke, has decided to leave your organization to take another position elsewhere. Due to the sensitive nature of the donor names and addresses on his personal tablet, you do not want him to be able to take that information with him to his next job. To prevent that from happening, you will remotely erase the account data from his device.

1. Export a list all the mobile devices in your domain.
    a) Sign in to the Admin console, if necessary.
    b) Select **Device management**.
    c) Select **Mobile devices** to display the list of devices in your domain.
    d) Verify that none of the devices are selected. Uncheck them, if necessary.
    e) Select the **EXPORT ALL** button.
       A compressed file named *yyyy-mm-dd*-**devices.csv** is downloaded to your **Downloads** folder.
    f) Open and view the exported file, if desired. You can refer to Figure 8-7 to see how the exported file looks in Excel.

2. Remotely wipe the G Suite account on the Android device.
    a) Return to the **Mobile devices** list.
    b) Select the Android device to be affected.
    c) Select **WIPE ACCOUNT**.
    d) When prompted to confirm, select **WIPE ACCOUNT**.

3. Use the **Mobile devices** page to remove the approved mobile device from your domain.
    a) From the Admin console **Home** page, select **Device management→Mobile devices**.

b) Select the mobile device to be removed.

 Note: Most likely, the name and email address attached to the device being deleted will be your name rather than "Luke" (from the scenario) or "Anna Son."

c) Select the **DELETE** button.

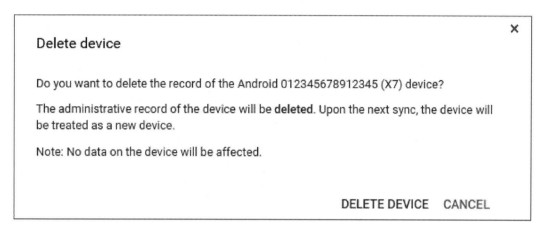

The **Delete device** dialog box is displayed.
d) Select **DELETE DEVICE** to confirm the deletion.
e) Refresh the browser page to verify that the device has been removed from your domain.

Summary

In this lesson, you learned about enabling users with mobile devices to access their G Suite accounts. And, to protect the content in your domain, you configured and enforced a Google Apps Device Policy so you can remotely manage the devices.

What types of controls do you want to enforce in your Google Apps Device Policy?

What are the dangers for allowing users to remote wipe devices?

 Note: Check your CHOICE Course screen for opportunities to interact with your classmates, peers, and the larger CHOICE online community about the topics covered in this course or other topics you are interested in. From the Course screen you can also access available resources for a more continuous learning experience.

9 Using Reporting Tools

Lesson Time: 1 hour, 30 minutes

Lesson Introduction

Now that your organization is up and running, your final—and ongoing—task as the admin is to maintain the functionality of the G Suite domain. In other words, you need to monitor the user and app activity to make sure that all is well and working as expected. When problems do occur, it's good to know which tools are available to help you troubleshoot and get things back to normal as soon as possible.

Lesson Objectives

In this lesson, you will:

- Monitor G Suite account activity and usage with reports.
- Track user activity with event-level details.
- Use the Email Log Search feature to view message details.

TOPIC A

Use Admin Console Reports

As time passes and your G Suite domain users go about their business, their activity increases and the amount of email messages and files begin to accumulate. You can use the Admin console reports feature to keep an eye on the activity and usage levels of the apps in the domain, as well as monitor the Google Drive™ storage and the apps usage.

Highlights Report

The first time you select the **Reports** control from the Admin console dashboard, Google provides a quick tour of the Highlights report. This report offers a birds-eye view of your domain. The **Apps usage activity** section provides information about apps activity over a selected period of time. Details about user status and how close they are to reaching their storage limits appears on the right side of the screen. The **Document visibility** section displays the number of documents that are visible internally and externally. This information along with the Security stats in the lower-right corner can give you a quick glance at how vulnerable your domain is from external documents and apps.

Many areas of the report are interactive and provide links to other reports when selected. For example, if you select the number of Active users in the right pane, the **Security report** page that contains the User Account Status is displayed. In the **Apps usage activity** chart at the top, you can hover over any date to display a detailed pop-up containing the number of apps used that specific day.

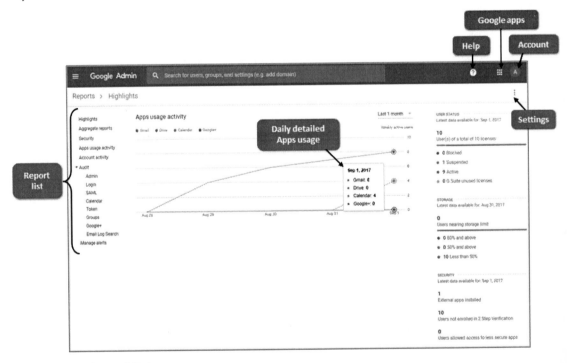

Figure 9-1: The Highlights report.

 Caution: The reports do not show real-time data and there might be a noticeable time lag for data to be refreshed.

Account Activity Report

At a glance, the Account activity report provides a list of users, including their account status and admin status. The top portion of the report provides a graphic representation of user account status over time. You can use the buttons in the upper-right corner to perform actions such as downloading the report data, changing the information that's shown in the report, filtering the data, and accessing help. These buttons are available and function similarly in other reports.

In the bottom portion of the report that contains the user list, you can use the **Columns** button to change the columns that are shown in the report. You can also use the column headings to rearrange the columns or change which column is illustrated in the chart at the top.

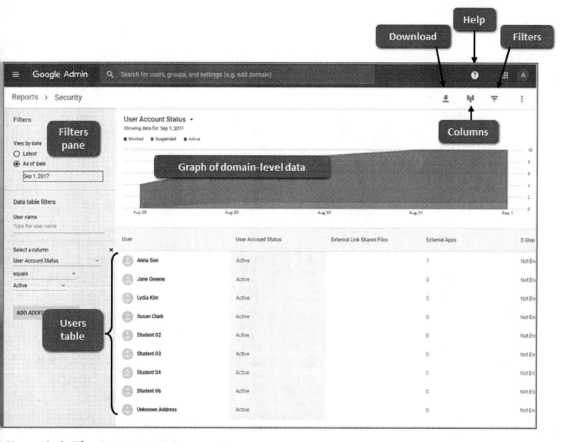

Figure 9-2: The Account activity report.

Security Report

The Security report provides details about the externally visible files, external apps, and users allowed access to less-secure apps. From this report, you can see which users make files visible to people outside of your domain and might be creating a vulnerability for sensitive or confidential information. If you are using the G Suite Business edition, then you also have access to the Drive audit log that provides details about when files were shared and which user shared them.

Also included in the Security report are those users who have not enrolled in 2-step verification. If you have enabled and enforced 2-step verification, you can use this report to know which users to contact and make sure they enroll in 2-step verification before they are locked out of their accounts.

You can access security reports from the **Security** menu on the left as well as the **Security section** links in the lower-right corner of the **Report Highlights** page.

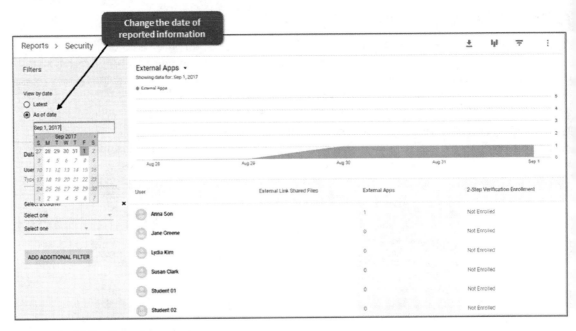

Figure 9-3: The Security report.

Apps Usage Activity Report

On the **Highlights** page, the **Apps usage activity** report displays the details about Drive files, Gmail™ usage, Calendar, and Google+ usage in your domain. This report can identify those users who are using the apps, as well as those who are not. Depending on the situation, you might need to alert the user if they're approaching their storage limit, or conversely, you might want to provide app training for some users.

You can select the Apps usage activity title to view user-level activity information. From the User table in the bottom of the report, you can select the data to display its details in the top chart. You can use the **Columns** button to modify the columns that appear in the User table. And, then you can use the column headings to sort and rearrange the column order within the table.

From the Highlights report, you can use the Apps usage activity chart to get a domain-level summary of how the apps are being used by users. In the upper-right corner of the chart, you can change the time period. You can select **Last 7 days** to change the period of time displayed in the report. As in other charts, you can point to a date in the chart to display the exact number of users using the apps that day.

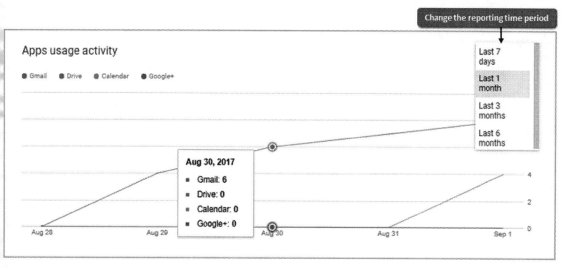

Figure 9-4: Apps usage activity report.

Disk Space Usage and Limits

In the Apps usage activity report, you can change the focus of the charted data at the top of the report. By default, it shows the number of files owned for the entire domain by app. The data shown in the columns (Files owned, Total Storage Used [MB], and Total Emails) is the data that is available to chart. Like the other reports, you can add and remove information from the report table by using the **Columns** button.

When trying to figure out how the disk space is being used, you might want to add columns and rearrange them in the report. For example, you might want to add the columns that give you more detail for the Drive app. The following figure shows the Apps usage activity report that has additional columns for the number of shared files and the number of uploaded files for each user.

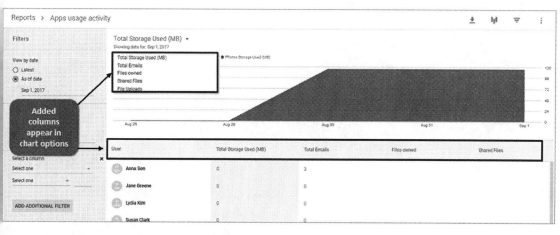

Figure 9-5: The Apps usage activity report.

Email Client Usage

You can use the Apps usage activity report and chart to identify the heavy Gmail users, as well as the total amount of emails being sent and received domain-wide. As you might expect, there are multiple ways to view Gmail statistics. From the Highlights report, when you view the last seven days in the Apps usage activity chart, the total number of emails exchanged is shown.

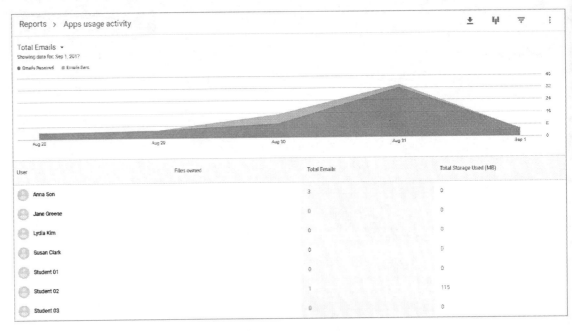

Figure 9-6: The Total Emails chart in the Apps usage activity report.

 Access the Checklist tile on your CHOICE Course screen for reference information and job aids on **How to Use the Admin Console Reports**.

ACTIVITY 9-1
Using Reports

Before You Begin
During Lesson 4, you shared the Donors spreadsheet with others.

Scenario
Your fund-raising committee chairperson just called in a panic. She was told by one of your largest donors that they had been approached by another organization who knew about their recent donation to Building with Heart. Knowing that the Donors spreadsheet exists, you immediately guess that someone inside of your organization has mistakenly sent the file to someone outside of your domain. Due to the sensitive financial nature of this file, you need to figure out how the document was leaked and prevent it from happening again.

1. Use the **Highlights** report to begin examining the data that has been collected about your G Suite domain.

    a) From the Admin console dashboard, select **Reports**.
    Because of the three-day lag time with the reporting feature, you won't have any reporting data to view. Direct your attention to the following figure or to your instructor's screen to see the interconnectedness of the reports.

b) Examine the sample **Highlights** report.

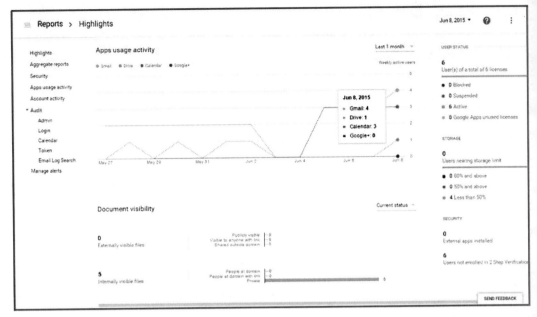

Note: Due to the cloud-based nature of G Suite, you might not be able to duplicate the exact content and format of the report used in this activity. As an admin, it's necessary to understand how to access the reports and interpret the data.

By default, the **Highlights** report is displayed and contains a summary of various statistics for the entire domain. You can select the numerical data to drill down into the details.

- The **Apps usage activity** chart provides a graphic illustration of how Gmail, Drive, Calendar, and Google+ are being used. You can change the time period of the charted data.
- The **Document visibility** section displays the number of files that are visible internally and externally.
- The **User status** section displays the number of users by status. This is helpful when monitoring the number of used or unused user licenses.
- The **Storage** section summarizes the number of users who are nearing their available storage limits.
- The **Security** section displays the number of external apps that have been installed and the number of users who are not enrolled in 2-step verification. You will want to monitor the latter number if you have enforced 2-step verification and need to make sure users are not locked out of their Apps accounts.

2. **If the scenario is to be believed and the sensitive Donors list was leaked to an external user, can the Highlights report help you begin to figure out who is responsible for the leak?**

Note: If you have a G Suite Business subscription, then the Externally visible files data is linked to the Drive audit log.

3. Examine the Apps usage activity report. What does this report indicate about how your domain users are using the apps?

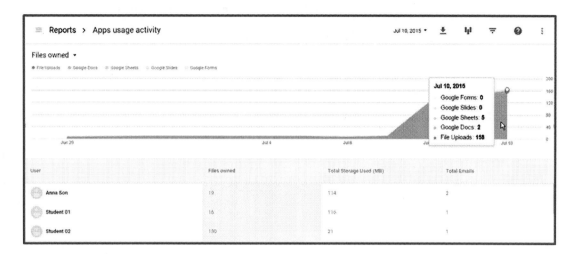

4. Examine the Account activity report. Does this report provide any unique information about the users in your domain?

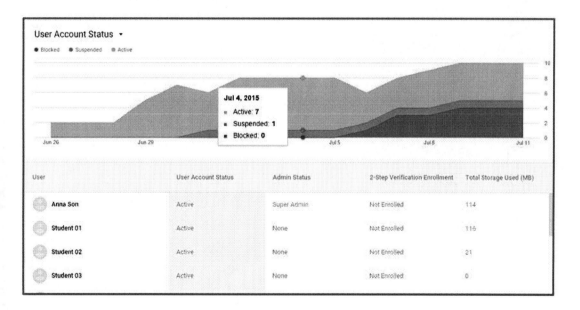

5. Do any of these reports show the files listed by file name?

_____

TOPIC B

Use Audit Logs

As the admin, it's your responsibility to stay on top of the events, especially odd or suspicious ones, that are happening in your domain. The audit logs can help you in this task by providing a variety of information about events that range from users logging in and out to your administrator's activities. It makes sense to look at the audit logs now that your domain is established and generating events to log.

Admin Audit Log

The *Admin audit log* tracks every event that happens in your Google Admin console and which admin performed the activity. Also included in the collected log information is an event description, date, and IP address where the admin signed in to the domain. You can show, hide, or rearrange the columns shown in the log; however, you cannot sort the log by column.

The **Filters** pane on the left can be used to display only those events that meet your selected criteria. For example, you might want to filter the log on events related to user creation to see who created a specific account. When you begin typing in the **Event name** field, a list of suggestions is displayed based on the first character you type. You can use the **Set Alert** button to monitor future events with the selected Event Name.

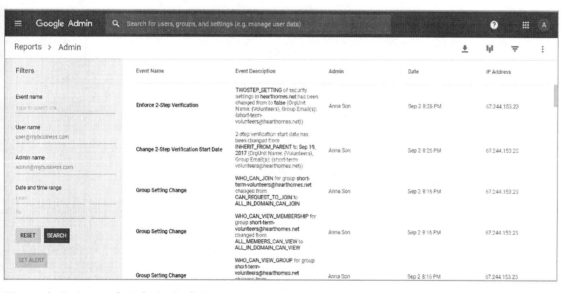

Figure 9-7: A sample Admin Audit Log.

Login Audit Log

The *Login audit log* tracks every web browser-based login to your domain and categorizes them as follows:

- Login Failure
- Login Success
- Logout
- Suspicious Login

Google defines suspicious logins as logins that are different from the user's normal behavior. Given the nature of cyber criminals and others who might try to gain unauthorized access to your domain, it's important to monitor and react appropriately to any suspicious behavior. As the administrator, when suspicious logins are reported, you should start by asking the user if they actually logged in from the stated location. Then, at the very least, you can reset the user's password. Additional, and more drastic, action should be taken if you're unable to verify that this suspicious login is legitimate. For example, you can use WHOIS to lookup the unusual IP address, and if it's outside of the expected geographical area, then you can treat it as suspicious.

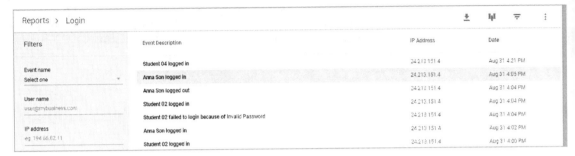

Figure 9-8: A sample Login audit log.

Calendar Audit Log

The *Calendar audit log* tracks events related to calendars, events, and subscriptions for your domain users. As calendar-related events happen, the entries should be posted within 30 minutes of the event.

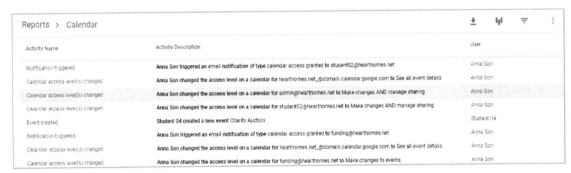

Figure 9-9: A sample Calendar audit log.

OAuth Token Audit Log

The *OAuth Token audit log* tracks every instance of a mobile or web application being authorized to access the data in your Google account. The log records the event description that reads as a statement, such as the first entry shown in the following figure, *"Anna Son authorized access to iOS Account Manager."*

Figure 9-10: A sample OAuth Token audit log.

Note: The OAuth Token Audit Log is simply labeled "Token" in the Audit section of Reports.

Manage Alerts

As the administrator, you can turn on alerts about specific events that happen within your domain. These can help you monitor domain activity and provide alerts to potentially harmful or destructive events, such as suspicious login activity. Google provides some built-in alerts that monitor common user activities. You can use **Reports→Manage alerts** to view and activate these predefined alerts. Alerts can be grouped into three categories: User, Settings, and Email.

- **User** alerts include suspicious logins, user password changes, Admin privilege changes, suspended users becoming active, and so on.
- **Settings** alerts monitor changes made to any applications or devices by an administrator using the Admin console.
- **Email** alerts monitor delivery events that include an Exchange journaling feature, a Smarthost failure, and a TLS failure.

You can also create your own custom alerts by using the **Filters** pane and the **Set Alert** button. By default, your custom alerts are automatically turned on.

Access the Checklist tile on your CHOICE Course screen for reference information and job aids on How to Use Audit Logs.

ACTIVITY 9-2
Tracking User Activity with Audit Logs

Data File
C:\093008Data\Using Reporting Tools\AuditReport-20150716.csv

Scenario
This morning, John noticed that some of the email messages that he received late yesterday afternoon have been marked as read. He knows that he didn't read these messages yesterday because he left early to play in a charity golf tournament. He'd like you to see if someone else has been logging in and reading his messages. You can start by checking the Login audit logs to look for suspicious or abnormal login behavior.

1. View the Login audit log.
    a) In the upper-left corner of the Admin console, select **Reports** to return to the main **Reports** page.

    b) Select **Audit→Login** and observe the listed events.
    You should see entries for successful logins and logouts. Event details include the user name, success or failure of the login, the user's IP address, and the date and time shown in your time zone.

    > **Note:** You can add the **Login Type** column to the log to see if the user logged in with their Google password or Single Sign On.

2. Download the Login audit log as a CSV file.
    a) Select and select **Download as CSV file**.
    The login audit log report is downloaded to the **Downloads** folder as a Comma Separated Values (CSV) file.

b) Open **C:\093008Data\Using Reporting Tools\AuditReport-20150716.csv**, the audit log file that has been downloaded for you.

	A	B	C
1	Event Description	IP Address	Date
2	Student 03 logged in	10.208.100.36	July 17 2015 2:14:24 AM
3	Student 04 logged in	24.240.115.4	July 16 2015 2:14:24 PM
4	Student 02 logged in	24.240.115.4	July 16 2015 2:13:53 PM
5	Student 01 logged in	24.240.115.4	July 16 2015 1:10:14 PM
6	Anna Son logged in	24.240.115.4	July 16 2015 12:10:03 PM
7	Student 03 logged in	107.14.166.70	July 16 2015 9:15:19 AM
8	Anna Son logged in	24.240.115.4	July 15 2015 8:06:22 PM
9	Anna Son logged out	24.240.115.4	July 15 2015 6:53:05 PM
10	Anna Son logged in	24.240.115.4	July 15 2015 2:39:57 PM
11	Anna Son logged out	24.240.115.4	July 15 2015 2:39:19 PM
12	Student 03 failed to login because of Invalid Pa:	24.240.115.4	July 15 2015 1:56:41 PM
13	Student 03 failed to login because of Invalid Pa:	24.240.115.4	July 15 2015 1:56:35 PM
14	Student 05 logged out	24.240.115.4	July 15 2015 1:59:05 PM
15	Student 05 logged in	24.240.115.4	July 15 2015 1:58:34 PM
16	Anna Son logged out	24.240.115.4	July 15 2015 1:58:12 PM
17	Student 03 failed to login because of Invalid Pa:	24.240.115.4	July 15 2015 1:56:41 PM
18	Student 03 failed to login because of Invalid Pa:	24.240.115.4	July 15 2015 1:56:35 PM
19	Student 02 logged in	24.240.115.4	July 15 2015 1:56:00 PM
20	Student 02 logged in	24.240.115.4	July 15 2015 1:55:32 PM
21	Anna Son logged in	24.240.115.4	July 14 2015 5:23:05 PM
22	Anna Son logged in	24.240.115.4	July 14 2015 5:02:15 PM
23	Student 03 failed to login because of Invalid Pa:	24.240.115.4	July 15 2015 1:56:41 PM
24	Student 03 failed to login because of Invalid Pa:	24.240.115.4	July 15 2015 1:56:35 PM
25	Anna Son failed to login because of Invalid Pass	24.240.115.4	July 14 2015 2:47:37 PM

AuditReport-20150716

3. When viewing the Login audit log, you see multiple failed logins by Student 03 at different periods of time. Are these repeated failed login attempts an automatic sign of trouble? Is there another indicator for whether or not this is normal behavior?

4. Now you see that after failing to log in several times, Student 03 was able to log in successfully as indicated in row 7; however, the successful login occurred from a different IP address. What does this successful login tell you? And, what's your next step?

5. Why is Student 03's successful login in row 2 potentially suspicious? What action, if any, should you take?

6. Use the Admin audit log to see what type of activity has been taken on Student 03's account.
    a) Close **AuditReport-20150716**. If prompted, do not save your changes.
    b) Select **Reports→Audit→Admin**.
    c) In the **Filters** pane, use the **Event name** field to search for **Student 03** events.

7. Has the user in question (Student 03) ever been suspended? Based on what you've seen in the audit logs, what actions can you take at this point to protect your domain?

ACTIVITY 9-3
Setting an Alert

Scenario

Now that you are aware of the suspicious login activity for Student 03's account, you can use the built-in alerts to make sure you are notified as soon as any events that might signal suspicious activity happen.

1. In the Login audit log report, add the **Login Type** column.
   a) Select **Reports→Audit→Login**.
   b) Select [icon] and then select **Login Type**.
   c) Select **APPLY**.
      You can now see how each user logged in to the domain.

2. Use **Manage alerts** to turn on the predefined **User deleted** alert.
   a) Select **Reports→Manage alerts**.
   b) Scroll to observe the available predefined alerts.
      By default, the predefined alerts are not turned on or activated.
   c) For the **User's password changed** alert, select the **Status** slider to turn **on** the alert (indicated by the blue color).
   d) Turn **on** the **Suspicious login activity** alert.

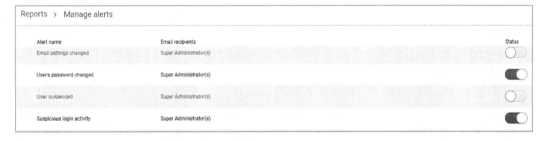

e) Select the **User's password changed** alert name to open the **Edit alert** dialog box.

The alert will be sent to all Super Admins in your domain and you can specify additional recipients, if desired.

f) Select **SAVE**.

3. **Use the Admin audit log to verify that the User's password changed alert is on.**
   a) Select **Reports→Audit→Admin**.
   b) Observe the **Alert Status Change** events that were recorded from your actions.

4. **Test the alert by resetting the password for Student 03.**
   a) Navigate to the Admin console **Users** page.
   b) For Student 03, select the **Reset password** icon.
   c) In the **Reset password** dialog box, type and confirm a new password.
   d) Do not check the option to require a new password at login. Select **RESET**.
       You can use the **SEND EMAIL** button to notify the user that their password has been reset. Of course, you will have to use an alternative email address for them to be able to view the email.
   e) Select **DONE**.

5. **Switch to the G Suite Admin's Inbox and read the alert that was sent.**
   a) Select   and then select the **Mail** icon.

b) Locate and open the new email from **G Suite Alerts**.

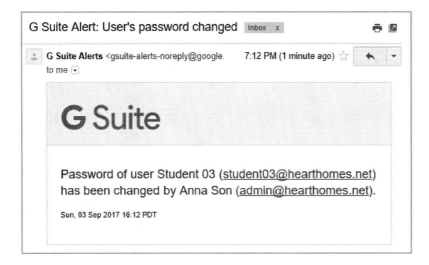

TOPIC C

Troubleshoot Mail Issues

Troubleshooting undelivered and lost email messages can take up a large majority of your administrative responsibilities.

Common Mail Issues

According to Google, some of the top mail delivery problems are ultimately caused by incorrect MX (Mail Exchange) records. If these record settings are wrong, then your Google mail delivery will be interrupted or stopped. You need to make sure that mail is being routed through the correct Google mail servers. To begin to correct the problem, navigate to **Apps→G Suite→Settings for Gmail→Advanced settings**. In the **MX Records** section, you can use the help link to open additional help documents. It's important to keep in mind that any MX records configuration changes can take up to 48 hours to propagate.

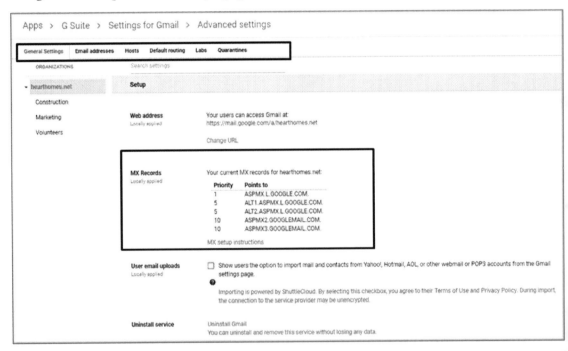

Figure 9-11: The tabs on the Gmail Advanced settings page.

 Note: For more detailed help and potential solutions to mail issues, go to the G Suite Administrator Help and search for Gmail service issues. Many of the help screens ask you questions to guide you to discovering a solution.

Some of the common issues reported by users in your domain might include:

- **Users are reporting that they are not receiving mail or delivery is delayed**. Some possible causes and solutions of this problem might be:
    - You might need to enable Gmail for your domain. Navigate to the **Gmail Apps** page to verify that Gmail is turned on.
    - If Gmail has been activated, then look into the accuracy of your MX records configuration and the email routing settings.
    - Verify if the user has exceeded their Gmail storage limit. If so, have them clean out old Gmail messages (**https://support.google.com/a/answer/1186436**).

- Depending on where the mail originated, your Google IP address might be on a suspicious list.
- On the other hand, verify that you have not blacklisted the sender's mail servers.
- Another cause might be networking problems.
• **Users are reporting problems with sent messages being delayed, not arriving, or bouncing**. To uncover the reason for the delay that users are reporting, it's useful to know the exact wording of the notification they receive. You can begin by having users verify that they've used a correct and valid email address. Additionally, you have a place to start troubleshooting if you can determine whether the delivery message was sent from the Mail Delivery Subsystem (mailer-daemon@googlemail.com).
• **User wants to send mail from a different address**. You can help users modify the "Send mail as" setting in their Gmail account to enable them to use an alternative address.
• **User wants to recover deleted email messages**. Deleted messages remain in the Trash for up to 30 days. You can help the user move the message from the Trash folder back to the Inbox. As the admin, you can restore a user's Drive data or their Gmail messages from the Admin console Users control.

The G Suite Toolbox provides several tools that can be used to diagnose problems and offer solutions.

- **Log Analyzer**—You can paste log text and run it through an analyzer to help interpret the log message.
- **Mail Message Header Analyzer**—You can paste email header text and run it through an analyzer to identify email delivery delays.

> **Note:** For additional information, check out the G Suite Toolbox web page at **https://toolbox.googleapps.com/apps/main/**.

Email Log Search

Available to Super Admins, the *Email Log Search* feature searches for messages based on a selected time period, sender email or IP address, recipient email or IP address, or the message ID. From the Admin console, select **Reports** and then select **Audit →Email Log Search**. When users report that they haven't received messages that they were expecting, or their messages weren't successfully delivered to the intended recipients, you can use the Email Log Search to investigate the problem. You will need to specify the date or range of time that you want to search and the sender's or recipient's names or IP addresses.

Figure 9-12: Using the Email Log Search.

After the search is complete, the search results appear at the bottom of the screen. Use the arrows to scroll through the multiple pages of search results. You can select the Subject or Message ID to open the Message details, as shown in the following figure.

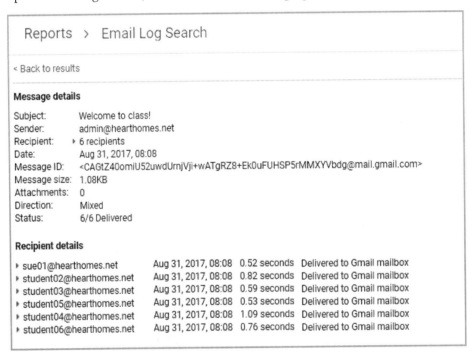

Figure 9-13: Viewing the Message Details.

The **Message details** section includes the subject, sender, recipient, date, message ID, message size, and the number of attachments. The **Recipient details** section also includes how long it took to be delivered to the recipient. You can select the arrow to expand the details and view the message's delivery path.

Guidelines for Troubleshooting Mail Issues

 Note: All of the Guidelines for this lesson are available as checklists from the **Checklist** tile on the CHOICE Course screen.

The following guidelines are provided to help you troubleshoot mail issues.

Troubleshoot Mail Issues

To identify and solve common mail issues:

- Verify that your MX records are configured correctly to use Google servers.
- Verify that you've enabled Gmail in your domain by selecting **Apps→G Suite→Gmail**.
- Verify that you have not blacklisted any incoming mail servers that would delay or interrupt receiving mail.
- If possible, verify that your G Suite domain hasn't been blacklisted by other domains that prevent your sent mail from being delivered.
- Use **Reports→Manage alerts** to turn on alerts regarding email events, such as the predefined "Gmail settings changed" alert.
- Use **Reports→Email Log Search** to search for email messages by sender name or IP, recipient name or IP, or message ID.
- Use the G Suite Toolbox to analyze the text of a log file or message header to help identify the problem.

Guidelines Dealing with Email Security

The following are some best practices for protecting your Gmail account and the valuable information contained in your email messages.

Deal with Email Security: Domain Users

Have your domain users do the following:

- Create a strong password that combines letters, numbers, and symbols.
- Change passwords often, especially if an account has been compromised.
- Never send passwords in an email. Trustworthy sites won't request passwords in this manner.
- Keep password reminders in a secure location or password app.

Deal with Email Security: Administrator

As the administrator, use the following practices to keep your G Suite mail domain secure:

- Enforce strong password creation and usage policy for users.
- Temporarily suspend suspicious user accounts and investigate the cause for suspicion.
- Immediately reset forgotten or lost passwords.
- When a user reports a lost device, immediately reset the user's sign-in cookies to end the session and force the user to sign in again.
- Ensure that users keep their recovery addresses up-to-date.
- Activate and enforce 2-step verification to provide the additional layer of security.
- Turn on account activity alerts so you're notified of suspicious login or service setting changes.
- Monitor users' login activity for suspicious or troubling issues.
- Monitor security reports.
- Monitor users' account settings and turn on account activity alerts so you're notified of suspicious login or service setting changes.
- Configure a DKIM record to provide authentication of outgoing email from your domain. (See Appendix A.)
- Configure an SPF record to identify your domain's authorized mail servers. (See Appendix A.)

- Configure a DMARC record to protect against someone forging the From address to send spam from your domain. (See Appendix A.)

ACTIVITY 9-4
Finding Messages with Email Log Search

Scenario
Last week, the director of volunteer recruiting sent a large number of email messages to prospective donors. Upon discovering that some of the messages didn't reach their intended recipients, you've been asked to figure out what happened to the emails and recover them, if possible.

1. Open the **Email Log Search**.
   a) Select **Reports→Audit→Email Log Search**.
   b) From the **Date** list, select **Last 7 days**.
   c) In the **Sender** name, enter **admin@<your_domain.com>**

   d) Select the **Search** button.
   A counter displays the elapsed time for your search.

    Note: An alert appears if the search results in more than 10,000 messages.

2. Observe the search results containing the messages that match your criteria.
   a) Scroll through the list.

   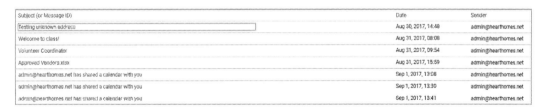

b) In the Subject column, select the message link for **Approved Vendors.xlsx** to view the Message details.

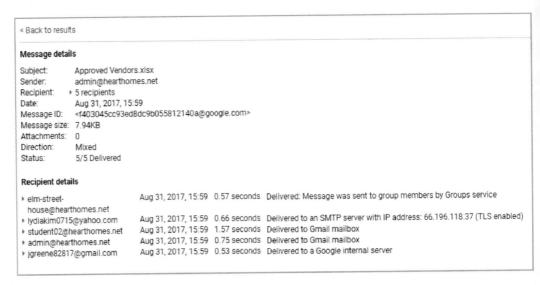

The Message details now display the message size and number of attachments. In the Recipient details, the duration to deliver the message is displayed, and you can view the delivery path that the message took.

c) Observe the five recipients displayed in the **Recipient details** section.
The individual recipients are displayed. The names displayed in your recipient list might vary.

3. **Download and view the search results.**
   a) Select **Back to results** to return to the **Email Log Search** page.
   b) Select the **Download** button and then select **Export to Google Sheets**.
   c) When download is complete, select **OPEN**.

The exported spreadsheet is named **LogSearchResults-***yyyymmdd-####* and every recipient appears in a separate row of the spreadsheet.

d) Scroll to view the information provided for each message.

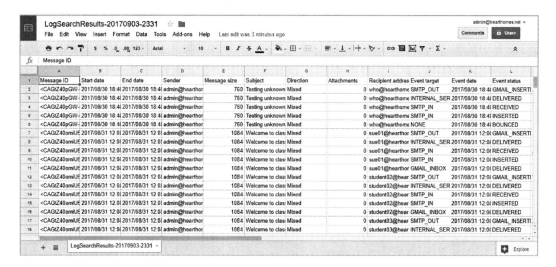

In addition to the details that were displayed on the **Message details** page, this exported spreadsheet contains additional information such as the target mailbox, the target IP, encryption status, and so on.

e) Close the exported log search results and the **Google Sheets** tab.

4. Return to the Admin console **Home** page.

Summary

In this lesson, you learned about the reports that are available to monitor account activity, apps usage, security, and audit logs for your domain. All of these reports provide information about events and incidents happening in your domain. You can use them to view how the apps and services are being used. Additionally, you used the Email Log Search feature to troubleshoot email problems.

What are some examples of how reports can be used to manage your domain?

Share some of your email troubleshooting experiences. Which experiences were the easiest to solve? Which were the most challenging?

Note: To learn more about getting support from Google, check out the LearnTO **Access Help from Google** presentation from the **LearnTO** tile on the CHOICE Course screen.

Note: Check your CHOICE Course screen for opportunities to interact with your classmates, peers, and the larger CHOICE online community about the topics covered in this course or other topics you are interested in. From the Course screen you can also access available resources for a more continuous learning experience.

10 Managing Domain Security and Authentication

Lesson Time: 1 hour, 45 minutes

Lesson Introduction

Although physical security of an organization's assets has always been a concern, there is a heightened level of concern with the security of organizational data. As the admin, it's your responsibility to make sure that the G Suite domain is protected. To secure your domain accounts and data, there are best practices to ensure that you have applied the appropriate security. Two-factor verification and single sign-on authentication and authorization methods are two available methods.

Lesson Objectives

In this lesson, you will:

- Manage the security controls in your G Suite domain.
- Secure the system by configuring 2-step verification.

TOPIC A

Manage G Suite Domain Security

In general, the security of your G Suite domain begins and ends with your users. From the strength of their passwords to how conscientious they are about sharing data, they can unintentionally open the door to trouble. As the admin, you have controls and policies that you can configure and monitor to ensure the security of your domain.

Domain Security

From the Admin console dashboard, you can use the **Security** control to view and configure security settings and policies for your domain. (Use the **Show more** command to display additional security settings.) Security and privacy are a big concern for administrators. You want to know that your accounts and data stored in the Google servers are secure and protected from tampering and destruction.

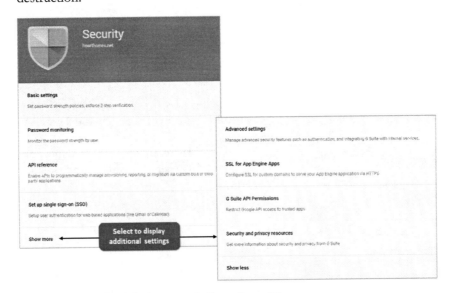

Figure 10-1: The Admin console Security settings page.

Authentication with OAuth

The *OAuth 2.0* protocol is used for authentication and authorization between a user's client application and a Google Application Programming Interface (API). It allows apps to access a user's resources without the user having to share their credentials. The Google Authorization Server handles the token request from the client, obtains (extracts) the token, and then sends it to the Google API.

The major steps for using OAuth to access a Google API are:

1. Obtain OAuth 2.0 credentials from the Google Developers Console.
2. Obtain an access token from the Google Authorization Server.
3. Send the access token to an API.
4. Refresh the access token, if necessary.

To manage your OAuth settings, from the Admin console dashboard select **Security→Advanced settings** and in the **Authentication** section, select **Manage API client access**. These settings enable you to control access to user data on applications that use OAuth protocol. Refer to the G

Suite Administrator Help documents for detailed information about using OAuth to manage API client access.

 Note: You have probably already experienced using OAuth tokens. If an app asks your permission to access resources such as contacts, location data, or other personal information, it is probably using OAuth tokens to do so.

Authentication with SSO

When users sign in to the G Suite domain with their user name and password, they are given access to the apps and services provided by their domain, such as Gmail™, Google Calendar™, and Marketplace apps. In general, *Single Sign-On (SSO)* is the authentication process that stores and shares user credentials between multiple applications and services. For example, a user can log in to their Gmail application and be automatically logged in to other Google web apps. This permits a user to log in once, and not be prompted to log in again as he/she accesses various services and resources. Google provides an SSO API based on Security-Assertion Markup Language (SAML) for you to use.

As the administrator, you can set up single sign-on from the Admin console dashboard by selecting **Security→Set up single sign-on (SSO)**. Setting up SSO requires generating public and private keys and an X.509 certificate that contains a public key, and registering the keys with Google. There are a variety of tools and utilities available for generating the necessary keys. The key-generation process will be different for each specific tool. Some of the available tools are:

- OpenSSL®—an open-source, command-line tool.
- Microsoft® Visual Studio® for .NET—a collection of tools.
- Keytool in Java™—a key and certification management utility.
- Java Cryptography Architecture (JCA)—an API that uses parts of the Java 2 SDK Security API.

 Note: For additional help and detailed instructions, see the G Suite Administrator online help at https://support.google.com.

 Note: To learn more about enabling SSO authentication, check out the LearnTO **Configure SSO** presentation from the **LearnTO** tile on the CHOICE Course screen.

Guidelines for Managing Security

 Note: All of the Guidelines for this lesson are available as checklists from the **Checklist** tile on the CHOICE Course screen.

Use the following guidelines to monitor and manage security in your G Suite domain.

Manage Security: Domain

In general, the following items are suggested as a way to keep your G Suite domain secure:

- Use 2-step verification to strengthen password security and prevent compromised passwords from causing harm.
- Use authentication methods to prevent spammers from spoofing email to look like it was sent from your domain.
- Monitor users' security settings and revoke application-specific passwords that provide access to a user account.
- Use the Admin console Reports to monitor user behavior and set alerts for suspicious activity.

Manage Security: User Accounts

In addition to the preceding security practices, this administrator's security checklist can be used to keep your user accounts secure:

- If user accounts become compromised, temporarily suspend the account.
- Immediately reset lost, stolen, or hacked passwords.
- Add recovery options so users can add secondary email addresses and phone numbers.
- Monitor the Login audit log for suspicious logins.
- Use the Security report to monitor potential data security issues for compromised accounts.
- Monitor user account settings and help them create strong passwords to secure their Gmail accounts.
- Enable account activity alerts to receive notification of an important or suspicious event.

ACTIVITY 10-1
Managing Domain Security

Scenario
You can monitor the user passwords in your domain to ensure that they are strong and provide enough protection. As the admin, one of the easiest password changes to make is increasing the minimum characters.

1. Open the **Security** control for your domain.
    a) From the Admin console dashboard, select **Security**.
    b) Expand the **Password monitoring** section.

NAME	PASSWORD LENGTH	PASSWORD STRENGTH
Anna Son	9	▬▬▬
Student 01	9	▬▬▬
Student 02	9	▬▬▬
Student 03	9	▬▬▬
Student 04	9	▬▬▬

   The password length and strength for each user is listed. You can quickly identify the users who need to strengthen their passwords. For users who have not signed in yet, there is password length or password strength indicators.

2. Knowing that users are the most vulnerable of the domain's assets, how can you prevent user accounts from being compromised?

3. For the entire domain, increase the minimum password length to **10**.
    a) Scroll up to expand the **Basic settings**.
       The default Minimum length for passwords is 8 characters.
    b) Edit the **Minimum length** to be **10**.
    c) Select **SAVE**.

4. How would you force users to change their passwords to conform to your password policies?

5. Select **Show more** and expand **Advanced settings** and observe the **Authentication** section.

   The **Authentication** settings can be used to manage the OAuth domain key, enable users to sign-in to third party websites, and give admins access to APIs that use the OAuth protocol.

    Note: As of May 2015, the Secure Data Connector is no longer available.

6. What is OAuth and how is it used to provide security in a G Suite domain?

TOPIC B

Configure 2-Step Verification

Requiring users to set strong passwords provides a basic layer of security for your G Suite domain. However, passwords can be forgotten or stolen. Fortunately, there are other methods that you can use to provide security. 2-step verification is one of these methods.

2-Step Verification

The process of *2-step verification*, based on the idea of two-factor verification, can increase the protection of your G Suite domain from lost or stolen user passwords and is one of the best ways to secure a mail account. When enabled, users will need to enter a verification code in addition to their user names and passwords to access their G Suite accounts. So, if a user's name and password were compromised, the verification code prevents someone else from gaining access to the user's account and domain.

Note: Accounts that use a SAML single sign-on (SSO) service can not enroll in 2-step verification.

When setting up 2-step verification, you will need to provide a primary phone number that can be used to receive a single-use security code—either text or voice. You have the option to check **Remember verification for this computer** so you are prompted to enter a verification code only every 30 days. However, if you log in using a different computer, or you delete your browser cookies, then you will be prompted to enter a new verification code.

Note: The Google Authenticator™ app can also be used on mobile devices to generate verification codes.

As the administrator, there are three primary steps that must be completed to turn on 2-step verification:

1. **Admin enables** 2-step verification for the domain.
2. **Users enroll** in 2-step verification by providing a primary phone number.
3. **Admin enforces** the security policy to make 2-step verification mandatory for all users.
   CAUTION: Only perform this step after all users have enrolled in 2-step verification, or you risk locking them out of their accounts.

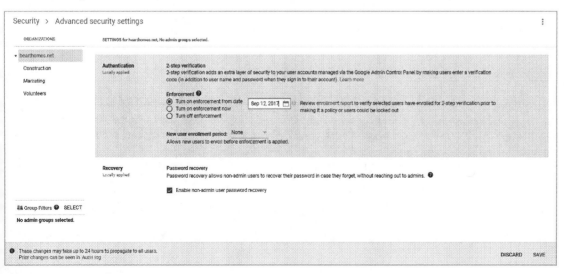

Figure 10-2: Turning on 2-step verification.

Backup Options and Backup Codes

If the smartphone that's been associated with an account for 2-step verification is lost, then you can sign in using backup codes. Like the verification code that you receive on your smartphone, the backup codes can be used only once. If you did not generate backup codes when you enrolled in 2-step verification, you can generate them now by selecting **My Account** and then selecting **Sign-in & security**. Navigate to the **2-Step Verification** setting to display the **Backup Options** shown here.

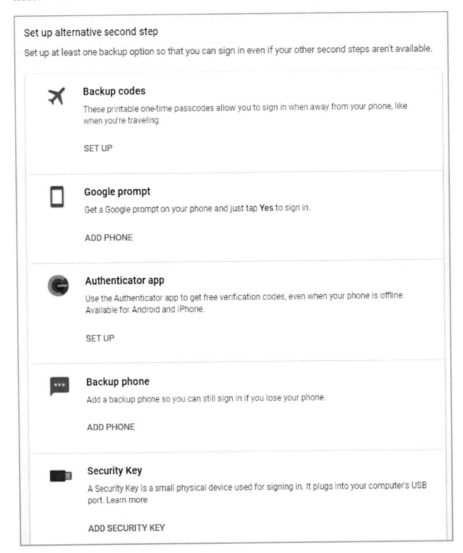

Figure 10-3: 2-Step Verification Backup Options.

From these backup options, you can add a backup phone number, print backup codes, download the codes to a text file, or generate new codes. If you choose to save the backup codes to a text file, the file name is *Backup-codes-<username.txt>* replacing *<username>* with your G Suite account name. The following figure illustrates how the printed backup codes will appear.

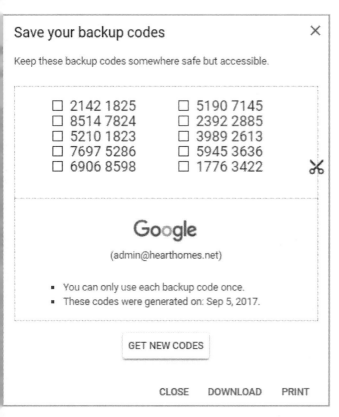

Figure 10-4: Sample backup verification codes.

 Access the Checklist tile on your CHOICE Course screen for reference information and job aids on **How to Configure 2-Step Verification.**

ACTIVITY 10-2
Enabling 2-Step Verification

Scenario

As the administrator of Building with Heart, you've decided to add the extra layer of protection provided by 2-step verification. You want to encourage everyone in your domain to enroll but it's mandatory only for the Construction organizational unit. Because many, if not all, of the users in the Construction group have been working in their domain accounts, it's important that you give them enough time to enroll. You'll want to notify everyone in the Construction group that they have one week to voluntarily enroll before they are forced to do so.

1. Use the **Settings** control to enable users in the domain to turn on 2-step verification.

    a) From the Admin console dashboard, select **Security**.
    b) Select **Basic settings**.
    c) In the **Two-step verification** section, verify that **Allow users to turn on 2-step verification** is selected.

    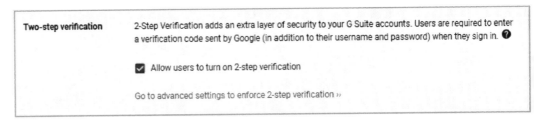

    d) If necessary, select **SAVE**.
    Your domain users can turn on two-step verification for themselves.

2. Observe the inherited security settings for the **Construction** organizational unit.

    a) In the **Two-step verification** section, select the **Go to advanced settings to enforce 2-step verification** link.

b) In the **ORGANIZATIONS** pane, select your top-level organization.

c) Observe the notification at the top of the page.

SETTINGS for hearthomes.net, No admin groups selected.

Changes to the **Authentication** settings will be applied to *<your_domain.com>* and no Admin groups have been selected.

d) Select the **Construction** organizational unit.
The Construction organizational unit inherits the **Authentication** settings from the top-level domain (hearthomes.net).

3. Enforce 2-step verification for the **Construction** organizational unit.

   a) Under **Enforcement**, select **Turn on enforcement from date**.

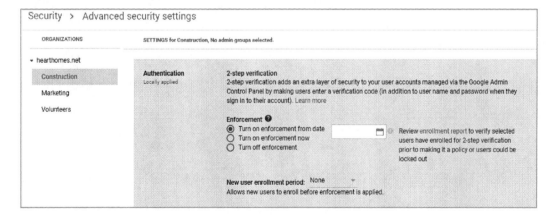

b) From the **Date** field, select a date next week.

c) Select **SAVE**.
The Construction settings are now locally applied while the Marketing and Volunteers organizational units continue to inherit their settings.

 Note: With Construction selected, you can point to the **Enforcement** settings and select the **USE INHERITED** button and then select **SAVE** to return to the settings applied to the top-level organization.

ACTIVITY 10-3
Enrolling in 2-Step Verification (Optional)

Data File
C:\093008Data\Managing Domain Security and Authentication\Backup-codes-admin.txt

Before You Begin
You have a smartphone to receive the security code by text or voice.

Scenario
As a member of the Building with Heart domain, you've been told that 2-step verification will be enforced across the domain next week. To avoid getting locked out of your account, you need to turn on 2-step verification and enroll.

---

1. For your Admin account, start the setup for 2-step verification.

    a) Select the **Apps grid** and then select **My Account**.

    b) In the **Sign-in & Security** box, select the **Signing in to Google** link to open the **Sign-in & security** page.

    > **Password & sign-in method**
    >
    > Your password protects your account. You can also add a second layer of protection with 2-Step Verification, which sends a single-use code to your phone for you to enter when you sign in. So even if somebody manages to steal your password, it is not enough to get into your account.
    >
    > **Note:** To change these settings, you will need to confirm your password.
    >
    > **Password**   Last changed: August 28, 10:21 AM   >
    >
    > **2-Step Verification**   Off   >

    2-Step Verification is currently off.

    c) Select the **2-Step Verification** setting to begin the setup.

d) Select the **GET STARTED** button.

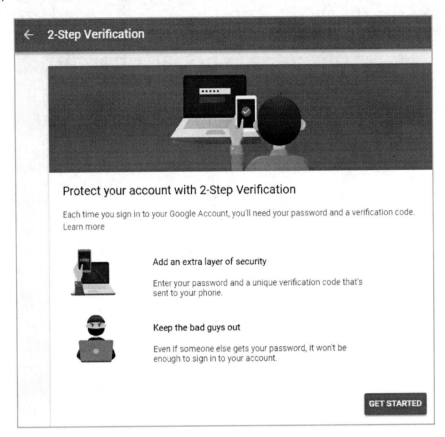

2. Follow the prompts to enroll in 2-step verification.
    a) In the **Phone number**, enter a number including area code. Select your preferred method for receiving security codes.

    A green check mark appears to the right of the phone number.
    b) Select **NEXT**.
    A verification code will be sent to the phone number you provided.

c) In the **Enter the code** field, type the code that was sent to your smartphone and select **NEXT**.

d) In Step 3 of the wizard, select **TURN ON** to complete turning on 2-step verification. The **2-Step Verification** page contains details about verification codes and also alternative backup options.

3. Explore the alternative backup options.

   a) In the **Backup Codes** section, select **SHOW CODES** to view the additional backup verification codes.

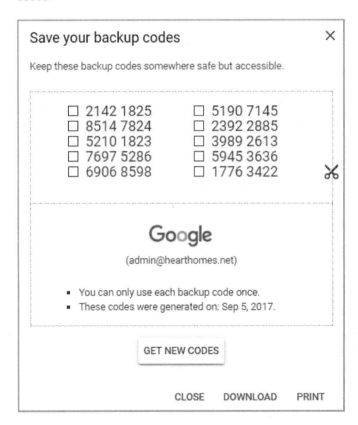

If you're unable to access your phone and need to enter a verification code to access your G Suite account, you can use one of these codes. Keep in mind that you can only use each code once. You can generate more codes at **https://accounts.google.com/SmsAuthConfig**.

b) Observe the alternative backup options.

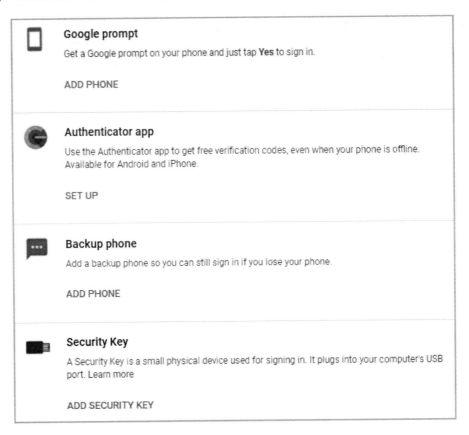

You can choose to receive codes by setting up Google prompt, the Google Authenticator app, a backup phone number, or a security key. All of these methods provide an additional level of assurance in the event your primary number is unavailable.

4. Turn off 2-step verification.
   a) At the top of the 2-Step Verification page, select **TURN OFF**.

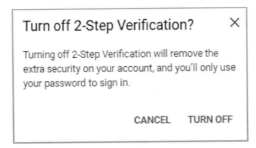

   b) Select **TURN OFF** to confirm it.

G Suite Account Deletion

The process to dismantle and delete a G Suite account is relatively straightforward. To start the process, you will delete user accounts, resources, and organizational units. Do not delete the Admin account. You will need to sign in as the admin to confirm the deletion. When you delete the user accounts, you will have the opportunity to transfer the data ownership. Once the users and organizational units have been deleted, you must cancel the subscription before the domain can be deleted. Finally, when all subscriptions have been cancelled, you can use the Company Profile page to delete the domain.

After deleting the domain, you must wait 24 hours before you can re-use the domain name for another G Suite account. If you were using the domain name with a paid subscription, then it might take up to seven days before the domain has been completely deleted.

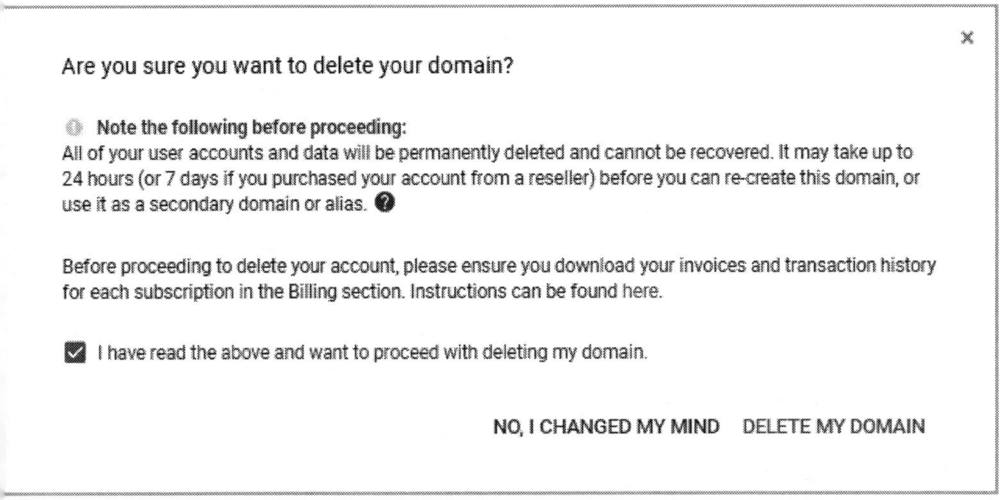

Are you sure you want to delete your domain?

Note the following before proceeding:
All of your user accounts and data will be permanently deleted and cannot be recovered. It may take up to 24 hours (or 7 days if you purchased your account from a reseller) before you can re-create this domain, or use it as a secondary domain or alias.

Before proceeding to delete your account, please ensure you download your invoices and transaction history for each subscription in the Billing section. Instructions can be found here.

☑ I have read the above and want to proceed with deleting my domain.

NO, I CHANGED MY MIND   DELETE MY DOMAIN

Figure 10-5: Confirming the deletion of the domain.

Access the Checklist tile on your CHOICE Course screen for reference information and job aids on How to Delete a G Suite Account.

ACTIVITY 10-4
Canceling and Deleting the G Suite Account

Scenario
After trying G Suite, you've decided to wait and get the legacy system in order before you migrate to G Suite. To make it possible for you to use the same domain name again, you need to cancel your subscription and delete the account. Then, when you're ready, the domain name will be available for you to set up again.

1. Remove the shared resources that were created for *<your_domain.com>*.
    a) Sign in as the Admin and go to the Admin console dashboard.
    b) Select **Apps→G Suite→Calendar→Resources**.
    c) In the **Resources** section, select the **Boardroom**, **Courtyard**, and **Mountain View** resources.
    d) Select the **DELETE RESOURCE(S)** button and select **OK** to confirm the deletion.

2. Remove the custom Building with Heart logo and replace it with the default Google logo.
    a) Select **Company profile→Personalization**.
    b) In the **Header logos** section, select **Default logo**.
    c) Select **SAVE**.

3. Delete all users in *<your_domain.com>*, but *not* the Admin account.
    a) From the Admin console dashboard, select **Users**.
    b) For each user (not the Admin), select the **Menu** icon and then select **Delete**.
    c) In the **User Deletion** dialog box, uncheck **Drive and Docs** and **Google+ Pages** to bypass the data transfer.

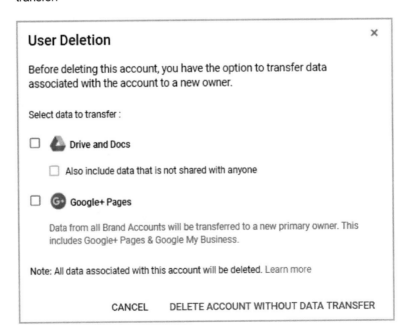

d) Select **DELETE ACCOUNT WITHOUT DATA TRANSFER**.
   e) Repeat these steps to delete all user accounts except the Admin account.

4. Delete the **Construction**, **Marketing**, and **Volunteers** organizational units for *<your_domain.com>*.

   a) On the **Users** page, for each organizational unit, select the **Menu** icon [:] and then select **Delete organization**.
   b) Select **OK** to confirm.
   c) Verify that only the Admin user account and the top-level organization remain.

5. Cancel the Google subscription.
   a) From the Admin console, select **Billing**.

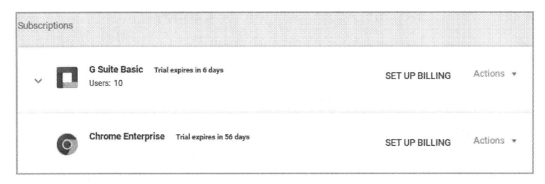

   Your current subscriptions are displayed.
   b) For the **G Suite Basic** subscription, select **Actions→Cancel subscription**.

   c) On the Cancel G Suite Basic screen, select **CONTINUE**.
   d) Select **Yes, I am sure** to confirm the cancellation process.
      You are now redirected to the Google **Sign in** page.

6. Delete the account for *<your_domain.com>*.
   a) Sign in as the Admin to *<your_domain.com>* and when the **Welcome to your account** page appears, select the **Accept** button.
      The **Company profile** page is displayed.
   b) On the **Company profile** page, select **Profile** to expand the section.
   c) Scroll to the **Account deletion** section and select the **DELETE THIS ACCOUNT** button.

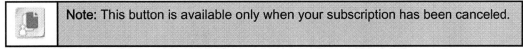

   Note: This button is available only when your subscription has been canceled.

   d) When prompted, select **I have read the above and want to proceed with deleting my domain**.
   e) Select **DELETE MY DOMAIN**.
      You are redirected to the G Suite website.

7. Close the Chrome web browser.

Summary

In this lesson, you learned about using 2-step verification and SSO for authenticating and authorizing user access to your domain. Although there are many topics about security, you scratched the surface by discussing some best practices for protecting your domain and enabling 2-step verification.

In your opinion, what is the biggest security concern for your G Suite domain?

Which authentication method do you find to be the most effective?

Note: Check your CHOICE Course screen for opportunities to interact with your classmates, peers, and the larger CHOICE online community about the topics covered in this course or other topics you are interested in. From the Course screen you can also access available resources for a more continuous learning experience.

Course Follow-Up

Congratulations! You have completed the *Google Cloud: G Suite Administrator* course. You have successfully set up a G Suite domain, navigated the Admin console dashboard, created users and organizational units, and managed mobile devices. You set up and managed mail delivery, routing, and filtering to enable communication within and outside of your domain. To facilitate collaboration, you have configured Google Drive and created Groups for Business so users can share files and work together. Finally, you monitored the domain by using reports and configured security to protect your G Suite domain.

What's Next?

Logical Operations offers several courses as a follow-up to this course, depending on your professional track. If you plan to develop apps to run on Google App Engine, consider starting with the *Python® Programming: Introduction* course and then taking the *Programming Google App Engine™ Applications in Python®* course.

You are encouraged to explore *G Suite* and the *Google Cloud* platform further by actively participating in any of the social media forums set up by your instructor or training administrator through the **Social Media** tile on the CHOICE Course screen.

A | Mapping Course Content to Google Certified Associate—G Suite Administrator

Obtaining the G Suite Administrator certification requires candidates to pass the Google Certified Associate—G Suite Administrator exam.

To assist you in your preparation for the exam, Logical Operations has provided a reference document that indicates where the exam objectives are covered in the *Google Cloud Administration: G Suite* courseware.

The exam-mapping document is available from the **Course** page on CHOICE. Log on to your CHOICE account, select the tile for this course, select the **Files** tile, and download and unzip the course files. The mapping reference will be in a subfolder named **Mappings**.

Best of luck in your exam preparation!

B | Incorporating Authentication of Your Email

Appendix Introduction

As the administrator for the G Suite domain, you have the added advantage of Google maintaining the mail servers to protect your organization from unwanted or malicious spam. Many of the email security settings are already configured for you, but can be modified to suit your organization's needs.

TOPIC A

Incorporate Authentication of Your Email

Knowledge of the following security practices can help you protect the messages sent from your domain. Email forgery and impersonation can undermine people's confidence in your company if spam appears to be coming from your organization. Use the following security techniques to validate your outgoing mail.

DKIM

DomainKeys Identified Mail (DKIM) is a digital signature that ensures the validity of the email sender. DKIM uses cryptography to prevent attackers from *email spoofing*, or altering email to look as if it was sent from your G Suite domain. The original message is signed by the sender or an independent signing service with an encoded, or encrypted, DKIM header. The receiving mail server uses the domain's public key to decode, or decrypt, the DKIM header and verify the authenticity of the email message. The DKIM signature enables your mail server to identify trusted mail messages that contain verifiable headers. As the administrator, you must configure a DKIM record first. The other signature validation techniques come after.

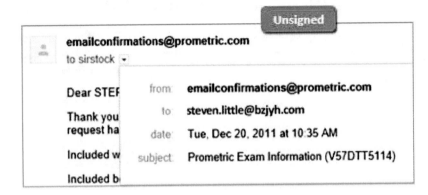

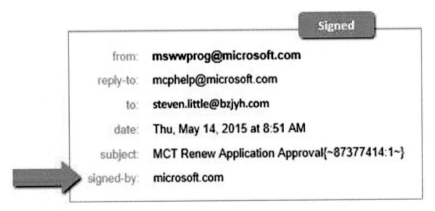

Figure B-1: An example of a mail header with a DKIM signature.

SPF Records

A *Sender Policy Framework (SPF)* record is a Domain Name Service (DNS) record that identifies which mail servers are authorized to send mail on behalf of your domain. Like the DKIM signatures, SPF records are used to prevent attackers from altering mail headers in an effort to impersonate someone from your domain. When a message is sent from your G Suite domain, the recipient's mail server will check the SPF record to verify that your Google server is listed as an authorized mail server. If the sending mail server is not found in the SPF record, then the message is rejected as spam. To avoid confusion, it's recommended that you create only one SPF record in your G Suite domain.

If you configure a gateway server for either incoming or outgoing mail, then you must include that gateway server in the SPF record.

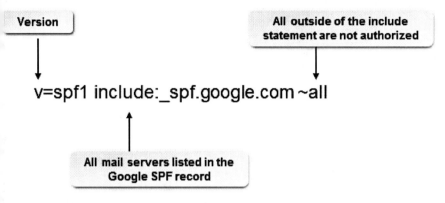

Figure B-2: The default SPF record.

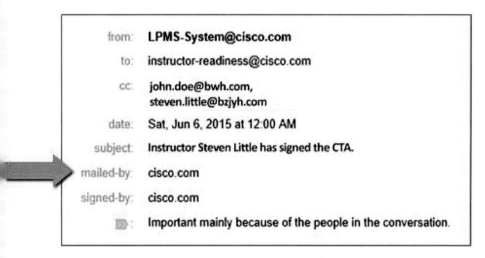

Figure B-3: An example of a mail header with a verified SPF record.

DMARC

Spammers and other cyber criminals can modify the headers of your domain email messages to make it look like their email messages are being sent from your domain. And, upon receiving an unauthenticated email, a user might fall victim to a phishing attempt and provide personal information because the user believed the email was legitimately from your domain. Sending spam from your organization can cause you to lose credibility and trust even though the spam wasn't intentionally sent by anyone in your organization. To prevent this type of spam, a collection of organizations created the Domain-based Message Authentication, Reporting, and Conformance (DMARC) technical standards. As the domain admin, you can configure SPF records and DKIM keys to maintain the signature integrity for your outgoing mail. Once the signature integrity is proven, then DMARC authenticates the messages.

You create a text record named **_dmarc.*your_domain.com*** that provides instructions on your DMARC policy. It's important that other organizations know your policy on how unauthenticated email from your domain should be handled. The three available policy settings are None, Quarantine, or Reject. It's recommended that you deploy the DMARC policy gradually until you're confident that all the legitimate emails are signed. Review the reports to monitor the email traffic and identify anomalies that might indicate email spoofing.

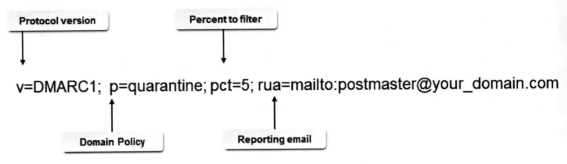

Figure B-4: A sample DMARC text record.

The following table contains commonly used tags in the DMARC text record. Only the v and p tags are required. All others are optional.

Tag Name	Definition	Sample
v	Protocol version	v=DMARC1
p	Policy for domain. Options include: • Quarantine: Messages are marked as spam. • Reject: Messages are stopped at the SMTP layer. • None: Only action taken is logging on the daily report.	p=quarantine
pct	Percent of messages subject to filtering.	pct=100
rua	Email address to receive the daily reports.	rua=mailto:postmaster@your_domain.com
sp	Policy for sub domains (relaxed or strict).	sp=r
aspf	Alignment to SPF. If partial matches are acceptable, then "r" for relaxed. If exact matches are required, then "s" for strict.	aspf=r

 Access the Checklist tile on your CHOICE Course screen for reference information and job aids on How to Validate Outgoing Mail.

Solutions

ACTIVITY 1-1: Planning a G Suite Account

1. **What domain name will you use? Do you currently own the domain name?**

   A: Answers will vary, but point out that you must verify that you own the domain name you want to use. If necessary, domain names can be purchased on-the-fly as you set up the Google account. And, when a domain is purchased, the MX records are automatically configured.

2. **Will you need to add a secondary domain?**

   A: Answers will vary. Based on this scenario, you probably don't need a second domain. However, if your organization does own multiple domains, you can add the other domains to your G Suite account so those users can have access to the apps and services.

3. **Will your domain need organization units within the top-level domain?**

   A: Answers will vary, but the logical way to organize a G Suite domain is to pattern it after the organization's structure. Based on the Building with Heart scenario, you might want to create organization units for Donations, Construction, Marketing, and Volunteers.

4. **How many users will you need to register?**

   A: Answers will vary. Right now, Building with Heart has only 15 staff members. The number of users that need access to your G Suite account will determine the edition that you purchase.

ACTIVITY 2-6: Resetting a User Password

3. **As a user, if you're unable to sign in to your Google account, what help is available to you?**

   A: Answers will vary, and will probably include contacting the Administrator. The other option available to users is the **Need help?** link. However, for this recovery service to work, some setup is required. You need to have a recovery email or phone number, and your Admin must enable this feature.

ACTIVITY 9-1: Using Reports

2. **If the scenario is to be believed and the sensitive Donors list was leaked to an external user, can the Highlights report help you begin to figure out who is responsible for the leak?**

   A: You might start by examining the **Document visibility** section in the Highlights report. The **Externally visible files** number refers to the number of files that users have made visible to others outside of your domain either by sharing or publishing to the web.

    Note: If you have a G Suite Business subscription, then the **Externally visible files** data is linked to the Drive audit log.

3. **Examine the Apps usage activity report. What does this report indicate about how your domain users are using the apps?**

   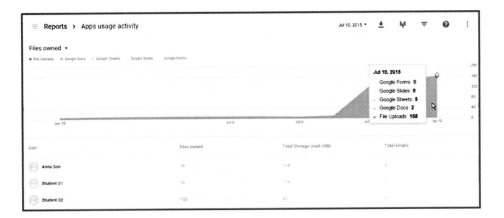

   A: The **Apps usage activity** report summarizes the amount of Gmail and Drive storage used by each user in the domain. If the apps usage is lower than expected, it might indicate that users are unfamiliar with the available apps.

Examine the Account activity report. Does this report provide any unique information about the users in your domain?

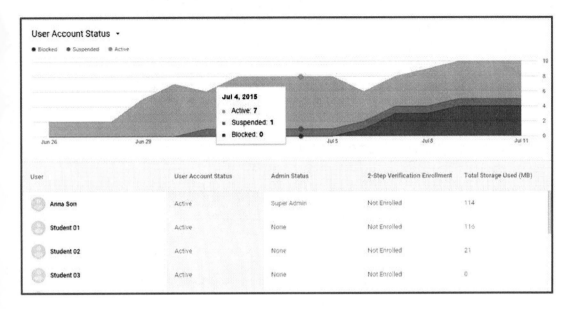

A: Like all G Suite reports, the data shown in this Account activity report can be customized to include the user data you would like to see. For example, you can see which users have Admin Status. You can add columns to include detailed information about each user's Drive and Gmail usage.

Do any of these reports show the files listed by file name?

A: At this point, the reports only show the number of files rather than the actual file names. If you have a G Suite Business account, then this data is linked to the Drive audit log that provides file details. However, if you are using a G Suite Basic account, then you'll need to find another way to search for the leaked file.

ACTIVITY 9-2: Tracking User Activity with Audit Logs

When viewing the Login audit log, you see multiple failed logins by Student 03 at different periods of time. Are these repeated failed login attempts an automatic sign of trouble? Is there another indicator for whether or not this is normal behavior?

A: Knowing that multiple failed logins can be a sign that someone is trying to gain unauthorized access to your domain, you definitely shouldn't ignore the situation. However, your first step might be to ask the user if they were indeed trying to log in and made typing mistakes while entering their password. Also, since the IP address of 24.240.115.4 is the same as the other successful logins by domain users, such as Anna Son, the user in question is most likely located at the office.

4. **Now you see that after failing to log in several times, Student 03 was able to log in successfully as indicated in row 7; however, the successful login occurred from a different IP address. What does this successful login tell you? And, what's your next step?**

    A: Because the IP address is different from your office IP address (24.240.115.4), you need to ask the user to confirm their location. While the different IP address might be potentially suspicious, the user might be working from home that day. So, a different IP address alone isn't always a sign that someone else is attempting to hack the user's password. After identifying the IP address that Student 03 is using, you want to look at the date and time stamp. In this case, the login occurred during normal business hours.

5. **Why is Student 03's successful login in row 2 potentially suspicious? What action, if any, should you take?**

    A: The different IP address is certainly cause for notice. Additionally, the date and time is outside of the normal time that Student 03 usually logs in. You need to ask the user if they were indeed logged in and then verify their location at this time. If this login event is outside of their normal behavior, you might want to suspend the user account to give you time to investigate the situation.

7. **Has the user in question (Student 03) ever been suspended? Based on what you've seen in the audit logs, what actions can you take at this point to protect your domain?**

    A: If the user has been suspended before, that might indicate that the user's account has been vulnerable before. You can suspend the user account and then reset their password and the sign-in cookies. This way, you've stopped the user's login session and forced them to change their password. You'll have to keep an eye out for the IP address that successfully logged in.

ACTIVITY 10-1: Managing Domain Security

2. **Knowing that users are the most vulnerable of the domain's assets, how can you prevent user accounts from being compromised?**

    A: As the admin, you can enforce minimum and maximum password lengths.

4. **How would you force users to change their passwords to conform to your password policies?**

    A: Go to the individual user's profile page and require the users to change their password the next time they sign in. Additionally, you can reset their sign-in cookies to instantaneously disconnect them from the G Suite domain and force them to sign in immediately.

6. **What is OAuth and how is it used to provide security in a G Suite domain?**

    A: OAuth is a token-based protocol that is used by developers to secure the apps that they create.

Glossary

2-step verification
Based on the idea of two-factor verification, requires users to enter a verification code after signing in with their user name and password to access their G Suite accounts. The domain admin must enable 2-step verification and can force users to sign up for it.

Admin audit log
The audit log that tracks every admin action and resulting event that occurs in the G Suite domain.

Admin console
The dashboard of controls that is used to manage a G Suite account and domain. It can be accessed by the admin from the **Google Apps** button or at **https://admin.google.com**.

blacklist
A list of IP addresses or email addresses that are blocked from exchanging mail with users in your domain.

Calendar audit log
One of the Audit reports that tracks events related to calendars, events, and subscriptions for your domain users.

Chromebook
A lightweight laptop running Chrome OS that provides access to the web and the common G Suite apps, such as Gmail, Google Drive, and the other Google productivity apps. It has a small hard drive for offline storage, but it's intended to be used while working online.

Chromebox
A physical box that can be connected to a monitor for video conference meetings. The Chromebox kit contains all of the necessary cables needed to attach an external monitor, a microphone, a web camera, and a remote control used to run all of the attached devices.

collaborative inbox
A type of Google Group that enables its members to track and manage the topic posts. Help desks and customer service departments commonly use this type of group mailbox to manage task assignments.

direct delivery
The default setting for routing Gmail in a G Suite domain. Incoming mail is routed directly to the users' inboxes. The opposite of direct delivery is modifying the Gmail settings to define an advanced configuration.

DKIM
(DomainKeys Identified Mail) An encrypted digital signature that is added to the header of an email to prevent spoofing while the email is in transit. Once decoded, the DKIM header proves that the message has not been altered during transmission.

DNS
(domain name system) The naming service used on the Internet that maps IP addresses to domain names.

DNS server
The computer that is running the DNS service used to resolve the DNS names with the IP addresses.

domain
A grouping of computers on the Internet based on the nature of their operations. Domains are identified by their unique names following the period in the web address, such as .com, .gov, and .edu.

domain alias
An alternate name for the primary domain that provides users with a second email address. For example, *user_name@domain.com* and *user_name@domain_alias.com*.

domain host
The Internet hosting service that manages and stores your G Suite domain records.

domain name
A unique name that identifies a domain on the Internet. Also known as site names, domain names are usually registered by organizations as their website address.

dual delivery
When incoming mail is routed to a Gmail inbox and a copy is also routed to a separate inbox. This is commonly used during a transition to Gmail from a legacy on-site mail server, or when an archiving mail server is used.

Email Log Search
A troubleshooting feature that is used to search for messages based on a selected time period, sender email or IP address, recipient email or IP address, or the message ID.

email spoofing
The act of altering the domain name portion of an email address to make it look like the email is coming from a reputable (or known) source.

G Suite
The all-in-one solution for an organization that provides access to productivity apps (such as Gmail and Drive), collaboration tools (such as Groups), and services on a subscription basis for everyone in your organization.

G Suite global directory
The directory of users in your G Suite domain that is integrated with Gmail, Drive, and Calendar so users can exchange email, share documents, and schedule appointments with other domain users.

GCDS
(Google Cloud Directory Sync) The tool that enables the admin to keep the Google domain directory synchronized with an LDAP server.

Google Drive
The cloud-based storage where all G Suite users save their files. Documents stored on Google Drive can be shared with users within or outside of your G Suite domain.

Google Group
The G Suite feature that enables users to create groups that are accessed from groups.google.com. Group members can discuss topics and collaborate by posting and replying to discussion topics, participating in a question-and-answer forum, and managing task assignments in a shared group mailbox.

Google Sync
The service that uses Microsoft Exchange ActiveSync to synchronize mail, calendar, and contacts between G Suite accounts and mobile devices.

group calendar
A calendar that has been shared with a group email address to enable multiple people to view and edit calendar events.

group-wide permissions
Assigned to "Anyone" and apply to all members and visitors.

IP address
(Internet Protocol address) A unique dotted decimal notation that is used to identify a computer or device, such as 198.175.10.4. Each decimal value represents the physical network, the subnet, network host, and device.

LDAP
(Lightweight Directory Access Protocol) A directory service protocol that connects over an Internet Protocol (IP) network and contains records of structured directory information stored on a server. LDAP is commonly used to provide a single sign-on for users to authenticate in the network.

login audit log
The audit log that tracks every web browser-based login to your domain and categorizes them as login success, login failure, suspicious login, and logout.

Mail Fetcher
The Gmail service that is used to import old messages and forward new messages as they arrive from an additional mail account so that you can work with mail messages from both accounts directly in Gmail.

mail gateway
A server that can be used to filter or archive your Google domain mail before it's delivered. By default, Google provides the gateway servers for your domain's inbound and outbound mail.

MX record
(Mail Exchange record) Stored on the DNS server, a record that contains information, such as the address of the destination mail server, the Time To Live (TTL) value in seconds, and record type, that is used to control incoming mail routing with Google mail servers.

MX toolbox
A powerful lookup utility (mxtoolbox.com) that can be used to discover a large amount of information about servers based on domain name, IP address, or host name.

OAuth 2.0
Protocol used for authentication and authorization between a user's client application and a Google Application Programming Interface (API). The Google Authorization Server handles the token request from the client, obtains (extracts) the token, and then sends it to the Google API.

OAuth Token audit log
One of the Audit reports that tracks every instance of a mobile or web application being authorized to access the data in your G Suite account.

organizational unit
A group created inside the top-level organization that can be used to group users and quickly assign rights and privileges to all users in the sub group.

primary domain
The domain name that identifies your G Suite account in email addresses and throughout the web.

Remote Wipe
The feature that deletes all content (apps and data) on a mobile device including the SD card and returns the device to the default settings. This feature can protect an organization's data and the device owner's personal information when the mobile device has been lost or stolen.

resource manager
A person who has been assigned the role of handling all incoming requests for a particular resource by accepting or declining on behalf of the resource.

role-specific permissions
Assigned to a role, such as "Member," "Owner," or "Manager."

shared resources
Calendar items that can be scheduled, such as meeting rooms, audio/video equipment, company cars, temporary office spaces, or lab equipment.

SPF record
(Sender Policy Framework record) A type of Domain Name Service (DNS) record that identifies which mail servers are authorized to send mail on behalf of your domain. The receiving mail server uses the SPF record to validate that the message is from an authorized mail server.

split delivery
When incoming mail is routed to a Gmail inbox or another inbox based on the email address, organizational unit, or some other criteria that is defined in the mail routing settings.

SSO
(Single Sign-On) An authentication process that stores and shares user credentials between multiple applications and services.

sub organization
See *organizational unit*.

web address
The textual name that identifies a site that has been reserved and assigned to a company, server, or file. For example, mydomain.com.

whitelist
A non-exclusive list of IP addresses that your domain trusts and accepts mail from.

Wipe Account
The feature that removes only a user's G Suite account information from a device and leaves the user's personal settings untouched.

Index

2-step verification *245*

A

Admin console
    overview of *11*
    Reports control *212*
    Security control *240*
Admin console reports
    Account activity *213*
    Apps usage activity *214*
    Disk Space Usage and Limits *215*
    Highlights *212*
    Security *213*
alerts
    categories *223*
APN *195*
Apple Push Certificate, *See* APN
audit logs
    Admin audit log *221*
    Calendar audit log *222*
    Login audit log *221*
    OAuth Token audit log *222*

C

Chromebook *189*
Chromebox *189*

D

device management
    Android for Work devices *195*
    Chrome devices *189*
    Device management page *188*
    export device list *206*
    G Suite Device Policy *192*
    iOS devices *195*
    mobile *188*
    mobile device activation *199*
    mobile device setup *196*
    Remote Wipe feature *207*
    security settings *192*
    supported mobile devices *189*
    Wipe Account *207*
DKIM *264*
DNS *4*
DNS server *4*
domain
    alias *2*
    defined *2*
    host *4*
    name *2*
DomainKeys Identified Mail, *See* DKIM
Domain Name System, *See* DNS
domain security
    Security settings page *240*

E

email spoofing *264*

G

GCDS *56*
Gmail
    Advanced settings *230*
    Attachment compliance setting *111*
    blacklist *107*
    Content compliance setting *111*
    features and settings *99*
    Inbox by Gmail *98*

Mail Fetcher *102*
manage quarantines *115*
migration to G Suite *119*
Objectionable content setting *111*
spam settings *108*
whitelist *107*
Gmail configuration
direct delivery *102*
dual delivery *103*
mail gateway *102*
split delivery *103*
Google Calendar
creating group calendars *168*
Google Cloud Directory Sync, *See* GCDS
Google domain
organizational structure *54*
Google Drive
app interface *72*
app settings *72*
automatic sync *76*
installation *76*
sharing configuration *84*
storage limits *78*
transfer of file ownership *89*
Google Groups
collaborative inbox *159*
group limits *143*
group settings *137*
Members list *134*
My groups page *132*
overview *130*
permissions *144*
roles *145*
sharing content *156*
types *132*
using Admin console *131*
vs. contact groups *131*
Google services *63*
Google Sync *196*
group calendars
calendar access *173*
overview of *168*
resource manager *180*
shared resources *176*
sharing methods *168*
sharing settings *168*
Groups for Business
overview *130*
policies *143*
settings *143*
GSMME *119*

G Suite
account deletion *254*
and Gmail *98*
billing plans *5*
Device Policy *192*
editions *12*
migration tools *119*
overview *2*
G Suite Migration for Microsoft Exchange, *See* GSMME

I

Internet Protocol address, *See* IP address
IP address *4*

M

Mail Exchange record, *See* MX record
Mail Fetcher *102*
mail issues
Email Log Search feature *231*
troubleshooting *230*
MX record *4*
MxToolbox *107*

O

OAuth 2.0 *240*
organizational units
adding users *55*
and device management *190*
definition of *54*
inheritance hierarchy *62*
organization structure
organizational units *54*

P

primary domain *2*

S

Sender Policy Framework, *See* SPF
Single Sign-On, *See* SSO
SPF *264*
SSO *241*
sub organizations, *See* organizational units

U

user accounts
admin roles *28*

creating *22*
deleting *34*
restoration *37*
suspension of *34*
Users page *22*
 passwords
admin password reset *47*
auto-generated *41*
management *43*
recovery *46*
resetting *40*
 Profile page *27*

 address *3*